POCKET LIBRARIES
NOT FOR RESALE

REDESIGN

THE

REALITY

OF

YOUR FINANCES

REDESIGN THE REALITY OF YOUR FINANCES

Understand the *Why* to Change the *How* of Your Spending

MARC BARLOW

Redesign the Reality of Your Finances:
Understand the Why to Change the How of Your Spending

Marc Barlow

Copyright © 2018 by Marc Barlow

ISBN-13: 978-1985316539
ISBN-10:1985316536

All rights reserved. No part of this book may be reproduced or transmitted in any form or by any means (electronic, mechanical, photocopying, recording, or otherwise) without written permission from the author.

For permission requests, email info@redesignthereality.com

Limited of Liability / Disclaimer of Warranty: While the author of this book has used his best efforts in preparing this book, he makes no representations or warranties with respect to the accuracy or completeness of the contents of this work with specific disclaimer of all warranties, including, without limitation, warranties of success for a particular purpose. The advice and strategies contained herein may not be suitable for your situation. The author shall not be liable for any loss of profit or damages arising herefrom. The author is not engaged in rendering legal, accounting, medical, or other professional services. If professional assistance is required, the services of a competent professional person should be sought. Further, readers should be aware that Internet websites listed in this work may have changed or disappeared between when this work was written and when it is read.

Praise for *Redesign the Reality of Your Finances*

"Marc's insightful and hope-filled perspective on getting out and staying out of debt and living a life full of gratitude is a message well worth reading, hearing, and sharing."
—Bob Goff,
author of *Everybody, Always* and the *New York Times* bestselling book, *Love Does*

"Marc takes a unique, yet practical approach in explaining the *why* behind the *how* of people's finances. By doing so, anyone can make even small changes and begin to stop the crushing downward spiral in their finances, and begin to see that there is hope of financial freedom for everyone."
—Craig Osborne,
Executive Pastor, Crosspointe Life Church

"This book's insights and tone will captivate and motivate you. Marc uses wise financial strategies and thought-provoking questions to help people explore the reasons behind their spending. Marc's book will inspire you to set new financial priorities and empower you to make decisions that reflect those priorities; thereby making redesigning the reality of your finances absolutely attainable."
—Danielle Womack,
Attorney, and Executive Director of La Mesa City Hope

CONTENTS:

Part One: *Why*

Chapter 1: The Why of This Book	1
Chapter 2: Tomorrow Begins Today	9
Chapter 3: The Debt Matrix	18
Chapter 4: Understanding the *Why*	27
Chapter 5: Your Biggest Asset: You	39
Chapter 6: Changing Trajectories, for Generations	50
Chapter 7: Mindsets	60

Part Two: *How*

Chapter 8: Developing Concrete Plans	72
Chapter 9: Discipline	80
Chapter 10: Eliminating Debt and Investing	96
Chapter 11: Learn to Enjoy the Journey	108
Chapter 12: How You Spend Your Money Matters	117
Chapter 13: Gratitude	132
Chapter 14: Practice Gratitude	146

PART ONE
WHY

CHAPTER 1: THE WHY OF THIS BOOK

ONE THING

There is a lot of information floating around the world. Websites, blogs, and books abound. So, what makes this book any different or any better? These are good questions. When I was a high school social science teacher, I taught a class called Life Management. Life Management covered a wide array of topics, ranging from self-esteem and communication skills, to budgeting, living on your own, writing a resume, and applying for a job. It also dealt with sexually transmitted diseases, stages of pregnancy, and parenting, as well as the negative effects of drugs and alcohol on the individual and society as a whole. As many people can personally attest, whether from their own memory of being an adolescent or from raising their own children, many adolescents believe they know more than they really do. I know I did.

So, while teaching such topics to students who were mostly 15- to 18-year-olds, I would always explain, "I understand many of you know a lot of this information already. However, you may have heard it during different stages or ages in your life. For example, hearing about the negative effects of drugs and alcohol in the fifth grade is a lot different than hearing this information in the eighth grade, and even more different in the eleventh grade. You have grown up and now have more experiences under your belt. Your experiences and insights can better anchor the information we are going to discuss. Therefore, I challenge you to take just one thing from this class and apply it to your life in a positive way. You never know—that one thing you learned and applied could save you thousands, or hundreds of thousands of dollars, or it might save you from a life of hardship and struggle. Perhaps it could even save your life."

I guess I would have to apply the same logic to this book. There may be one sentence, one chapter, an explanation, a concept, or a suggestion that strikes a particular chord with you. Maybe it will be something you heard once before, but, now, under different circumstances, you hear it differently. Now it just makes sense. Therefore, you receive it and apply it to your life in a positive way.

I guess, then, it is you, the individual person, that makes this book different from any other form of information floating around the world: how you interpret, perceive, receive, and apply what you read, hear, and learn. In this regard, I appreciate Aristotle's view of information when he said, "It is the mark of an educated mind to be able to entertain a thought without accepting it."

BACKGROUND

My wife and I have been married 27 years, and we have two amazing adult children. Both our children just graduated college, where we paid cash for their tuition and books. We own a modest home, and, as a family, embarked on 25-day road trips across the United States and into Canada. In recent years, my wife and I have experienced a 24-day adventure through Europe; an 18-day escapade to Japan; and a 28-day trek through England, Ireland, Scotland, and Wales. I feel my life is good. However, as you know, life is not always easy. Although we are in a different reality now, my wife and I struggled financially for many years.

My wife and I got married and had children at a young age—19 and 20, respectively. For the first five years of our marriage, we received government assistance in the form of health insurance and food stamps as I diligently pursued my college education. Knowing I could not raise a family as a busboy, I worked extremely hard to graduate from college within four years, get my teaching credential, and find a job as a social science teacher. Even after being blessed with a teaching job, we continued to struggle financially. Although my wife's part-time earnings as a hair stylist helped, being a new teacher did not provide a lot of money while trying to provide for a family of four.

However, in all honesty, many of the decisions my wife and I made during this time directly and negatively affected our financial situation. We struggled financially—not because of a lack of money—but because of a lack of discipline. As I will explain in Chapter 9, discipline is the key to redesigning the reality of your finances. After slowly realizing the insanity of our decision-making processes and our systems of spending (we were living well beyond our means on credit), my wife and I finally became disciplined and took control of our finances by adopting a long-haul perspective. Therefore, we addressed, dealt with, and created concrete plans related to the topics discussed in this book.

Over time, and by working hard to be more disciplined, my wife and I began to live within our means, prioritize our purchases, and eliminate most of our debt. By doing so, we reduced the stress and anxiety that often accompanies excessive debt and learned to be content, mindful, and present. Using cash instead of credit, we were able to take incredible vacations, pay for our kids' college educations, and started investing in our future. These actions were accomplished by the decisions we actively made, not necessarily by the amount of money we had.

I have worked with other educators whose spouses were either in education or in other professions. They couldn't believe it when I would tell them about the three-to four-week trips my wife and I were planning, or how we paid cash for our kids' college. Yes, many of these people had nicer houses, drove nicer cars, and had nicer things.

However, all those nicer possessions came at a price.

By developing the long-haul perspective and becoming more disciplined, my wife and I agreed that having experiences and being financially free were more important than having nicer "things." We agreed that our kids would remember the trips and adventures we had taken when they were younger, far more than a beautiful modern kitchen.

We also agreed that being mindful—by being physically and mentally present—on a daily basis for our kids and for each other, and being financially free, were more essential than living under the constant stress and anxiety from the accumulation of excessive debt due to purchasing things on credit. Finally, we agreed that pursuing vital life goals was more important than having to work extra hard to pay for nicer things, like a fancy new car. So, my wife quit her job as a hair stylist to pursue other artistic interests. In the end, what separated my wife and me from a lot of people we knew was our life decisions and how we used our money, and not necessarily how much money we had.

It is incredibly liberating to be financially free. Using the long-haul perspective and greater self-discipline, my wife and I have found we have breathing room. And although we are not yet 100 percent debt free (we still have a mortgage), we are well on the road to that goal. We are in a place where that reality is on the horizon. Having navigated my family's finances successfully through the ups and downs of life, I have also turned to assist other families in redesigning the reality of their finances as well. In addition to having learned from dealing with our own household expenses, I have had other training that has helped.

As a high school assistant principal, I managed and oversaw over $1 million in state and federal funds. Then, as a district-level administrator, I managed and oversaw over $7 million in state and federal funds, and successfully guided the district through multiple state and federal audits of its various programs. Many of the principles I have learned, refined, and benefited from both personally and professionally are presented in this book.

By American standards, I am by no means wealthy. However, by world standards, and how most other people live around the world, I am a millionaire. And, believe it or not, so are you. As will be discussed at the end of this book, being grateful is at the heart of being successful. Therefore, through honest reflection, being able to define what success means to you will be critical. As part of the success equation, for me, money has little to do with true "success." Rather, I equate success to an experience my wife and I had not long ago.

On a beautiful, clear December day, when it was about 75 degrees, our son and his girlfriend, our daughter and her boyfriend, and my wife and I went on a walk through numerous charming neighborhoods on the outskirts of downtown San Diego. We all ate lunch together, went to a bar for some drinks, and then ended up at a place that served pretzels and craft beer.

While there, we all went around the table and said what we were thankful for, appreciated, and admired the most about each person. That seven-hour period spent in the company of the people I love is what encapsulates success for me. At that moment, I felt I was the most successful man in the world.

That day, I was thankful for my family and the relationships we have that allowed us to share times like this together. I was thankful for our health, which allowed us to take a six-mile walk together. I was thankful for my job in education that not only allowed me to support my family but also provided me ample time off. I was thankful for the freedom and protection provided to me by living in the United States. I was thankful for living specifically in San Diego, where I could go on a long, leisurely walk in the middle of December wearing just shorts and a T-shirt. Finally, and most importantly, I was thankful to God for allowing me to experience this life, my life, in all its wonder. Even though life can be quite difficult at times, life can be exceptionally good.

AUDIENCE FOR THIS BOOK

Although far from perfect, living in the United States is truly a blessing. This country has provided me a great deal, and I have much to be thankful for. However, living in the United States can also be extremely complex, especially if you have assets (i.e., vehicles, property, investments, and capital). Therefore, I always recommend speaking with experts in fields like insurance, tax, investment, wills and trusts, and other areas that can affect your assets.

Every person and each situation is different. This book, for example, is not for people wanting to expand their investment portfolio, nor is it for those needing to know which type of insurance to buy and at what amounts. Although I will speak from a bird's-eye view on such topics, advice on exactly how to proceed with such things should be sought from trusted experts in their fields.

Before I sat down to write this book, I did some in-depth research on books on personal finance. During this process, I read many reviews of other books to see what people liked and did not like. Approximately one to six percent of people who provided reviews of various personal finance books gave the book they had just read only one or two stars out of five. In reading these one- and two-star comments, people spoke about the length of the book being too long and drawn out; that the information was either too basic or too complex; and that they were expecting an exact plan of action to become debt free or wealthy, which the book did not provide, just to name a few of the criticisms.

Knowing that one book could never fully satisfy the needs of all people, my conclusion from reading the numerous reviews was, simply put, that different people perceive things differently. This conclusion is evident throughout history. As a social science teacher, I attempted to illustrate this conclusion to my students in a rather unorthodox way.

I taught tenth-grade world history for ten years. On the first day of school, as soon as the bell rang, and after introducing myself, I would walk around the front of the room acting anxious, pretending like I was not prepared to teach. After several minutes of this charade, I would falsely confess that I was not prepared, but would still need to take roll. After taking roll, once again, I would fumble around the front of the room for several minutes, allowing the students to think we were done for the day.

As they began to talk among themselves, I would "accidentally" trip over a trash can, sending it screaming into the wall, while falling on, and then rolling off my desk onto the floor. Finally, I would get up slowly, with a grimacing look on my face, holding one of my legs in pain, and limp out of the classroom. As one can imagine, the class was shocked into silence as the students tried to figure out what had just happened.

After waiting outside for a minute or so, I would limp back in and tell the students I was okay, but a little embarrassed. Regaining my composure, I would explain that since I was not prepared for the day, we could use what just happened to learn about history. I would tell them to pretend I had hit my head and died during the fall and that the police had come to investigate, wanting a detailed statement from each of them. I know it was a morbid scenario, but I wanted them to take it seriously, which they always did.

After students wrote what they saw or heard—or what they thought they saw or heard—I would explain they were, in fact, writing history: they were writing different views and interpretations of an event. I would further explain that people's views and interpretations are based on their varying life experiences, which allows two people to experience the same event quite differently. Once again, different people perceive things differently. The same holds true for this book and the people who read it: every person's situation is unique, and their needs and wants will be distinctive.

With this clearly in mind, then, the goal of this book is to help people redesign the reality of their finances by unplugging from the debt matrix to live a more liberated life. This is to be a life free from the chronic stress and anxiety caused by excessive debt. Using deep, honest reflection, this book can provide a road map for people to follow to get themselves out of debt, stay out of debt, and become financially free. Then, once out from under the excessive debt shadow, they can plan for a brighter financial future.

CHAPTER 2: TOMORROW BEGINS TODAY

THE "MYTH OF ADOLESCENCE"

Growing up in the suburbs of San Diego, California during the eighties was a blast. However, my parents did not believe in giving me rides anywhere; all requests were met with the same response, "Ride your damn bike!" Therefore, I rode my bike everywhere. As young as ten years old, I would leave my house around 8:00 a.m., and would not return until well after the sun went down. There were no cell phones to track my whereabouts. I was on my own, and it was awesome: every day was another adventure.

One day, when I was about 13 years old, my friends and I decided to ride our bikes to Mission Beach. Taking side streets, Mission Beach was about a 25-mile bike ride from where I lived. While riding over the Mission Bay Bridge toward Mission Beach, I had the "brilliant" idea of jumping off the bridge. So, being the idiotic daredevil of the group—my antics had been greatly escalating in danger over the years—I jumped off my bike and climbed over the bridge railing. Being a young teenage boy, and being ignorant and naïve regarding just about anything and everything, I let go of the railing and dropped about 60 feet into the Mission Bay waters.

As the weight of my torso began to take me backward in my descent, I frantically flapped my arms back and forth in an effort to avoid landing on my back. As a result, when I finally hit the water, I was in a sitting position. I received an instant enema. As I limped out of the water, a man with a camera who witnessed the stupidity screamed, "That was awesome! Do it again so I can take some pictures." Again, being a thirteen-year-old boy, I agreed.

Thus, I climbed up and over the railing again, holding it with my arms behind me in order to lean out over the water as much as possible. My goal was to drop in such a way as to keep me from landing in that same enema-producing, seated position. My new strategy worked. I dropped perfectly and hit the water feet first. It was exhilarating. It was such a rush that I decided to do it yet again. However, this time, as I was running back to my jumping point, some vital information was able to penetrate my adolescent brain.

Mission Bay Bridge is a wide bridge, having four lanes: two lanes heading into Mission Beach and two lanes exiting the beach. As this revelation hit me, I realized that hundreds of boats traveling into and away from the Mission Bay waters might possibly be coming toward me as they entered or exited the area under the bridge where I was jumping. I might easily crash onto a boat as it passed below. Yet, again, being a 13-year-old boy, instead of stopping and counting my blessing for not having died, I decided to trust another boy my age; I asked him to go to the other side of the bridge and tell me when it was clear.

As I held the railing, again hanging out and over the water, my friend yelled, "Okay, clear! Go for it!" For some reason, something in me hesitated; during the two prior jumps, I had simply climbed over the railing without thinking and just let go. However, this time, I paused. While I was there, hesitating, a large yacht passed right below where I would have landed had I let go. I quickly climbed back over the railing and yelled at my friend, "What were you thinking?!" The look of panic and sheer terror on his face expressed to me that my young teenage friend was just that: another 13-year-old boy who did not know what he was doing.

This is the epitome of what I would later refer to while teaching my course Life Management to high school students as "the myth of adolescence"—it is the belief that "it" won't happen to me. "It" being teenage pregnancy, drug addiction, sexually transmitted diseases, injuring or even killing someone by drinking and driving, or, in this case, becoming paralyzed, or even dying while jumping off the Mission Bay Bridge.

Unfortunately, there are many people living out the "myth of adolescence" in their adult lives as well. Decisions have long-term effects. Some of these decisions are related to how people view and use money. However, no matter where you are in life, no matter the severity of the decisions you have made, and no matter what your present condition is, there is always hope. Tomorrow is another day. Tomorrow provides a redo. Tomorrow is its own reality. Although a cliché, clichés can be true: "Tomorrow is the first day of the rest of your life."

FREEDOM OF CHOICE, NOT OF CONSEQUENCES

In today's world, via the Internet, an almost infinite amount of information is literally at people's fingertips. Some information is accurate. Some information is inaccurate. Some information is research-based and objective. Some information is opinion-based and subjective. Regardless of the type of information people access, acquiring information is not the same as applying information. Information is only as good as the way in which people apply it.

If good information is applied properly, there are many issues, problems, and conditions in people's daily lives that can be resolved. For example, a person need not read study after study to know that eating fast-food and living a sedentary lifestyle can have negative effects on one's health. Yet, how many people do not take what they know to be true and apply it in their lives? In many cases, but not all, information is not what is lacking. What lies deeper, at the root, is *why* people ignore, fail, or choose not to apply such information in order to live better, healthier lives. The same can be said about the reasons *why* people spend their money in the ways that they do.

Right thinking is the raw material for right actions. People's actions will naturally reveal the direction of their thoughts. So, what are your thoughts about money? And more specifically, what are your thoughts about *your* money? Do you, or can you, envision yourself in five, ten, fifteen, twenty, thirty, forty, fifty, or even sixty years from now? What does your life look like at those different ages? Who are you with? What are you doing? How are you spending your time and money? Finally, how aligned are your thoughts about such questions with your current actions? With the average life expectancy of Americans being approximately 79 years, both envisioning yourself later in life and planning for your future are quite important.

However, this is where the tension lies—between enjoying yourself in the present moment, and being aware of and planning for your future. Although tomorrow is promised to no one, statistically speaking, if you are, say, 20 years old, you still have 21,535 tomorrows (79 years - 20 years = 59 years. 59 years x 365 days = 21,535 tomorrows). Therefore, today's actions affect tomorrow's reality. We have freedom of choice, but not of consequences.

We cannot eat fast-food and live a sedentary lifestyle and then choose what type of negative health effects those decisions will have. We cannot say, "Okay, I am willing to have higher blood pressure, but I'll skip type 2 diabetes." The same holds true for money. We cannot spend all our money enjoying ourselves in the present moment, and then expect our tomorrows to be better off than our todays. Therefore, the first step in planning for your future is protecting yourself, your loved ones, and your assets today.

FIRST THINGS FIRST: INSURANCE

The main principle to keep in mind about any and all types of insurance is this: insurance allows you to transfer your risk and your liability to someone else. Without insurance—whether it be life, health, home, auto, or rental—the risks and liabilities are yours and yours alone. Therefore, do not fall victim to the "myth of adolescence" by thinking "it" won't happen to me. In all reality, unfortunately, "it" happens to people every second of every day.

One spring, my wife and I took a vacation to Palm Springs, California. While preparing dinner, my wife sliced open the palm of her hand, requiring immediate medical attention. We contacted the front desk, and they told us where the nearest hospital was. Quickly, we jumped into the car and sped to the emergency room. While in the ER, the attending doctor wanted to take an X-ray to make sure there was no deeper tissue damage. Once the X-ray confirmed that this was the case, the doctor brought in a suture kit and stitched up my wife's hand. Unbelievably, we were at the hospital for only an hour and a half.

If being pregnant and giving birth to two children did not reveal how tough my wife was, then slicing her hand open surely did. She was cool, calm, and collected during the entire ordeal. Although we were not covered by the hospital we went to, we did have health insurance, so the hospital got our health insurance information to bill our provider for their services. Several months later, our health insurance provider contacted us to confirm the bill. I was amazed at how much the hospital charged for the emergency room service: $4,000 for an emergency room visit with an X-ray and stitches. We were astounded…$4,000!

HEALTH INSURANCE

Imagine if we did not have health insurance. That vacation to Palm Springs would have gone from $1,000 to $5,000 within an hour and a half. Not only that, but we would have had nothing to show for the $4,000 except for a scar. Furthermore, as will be discussed in Chapter

6, that $4,000 would have been the cost of five semesters' worth of books for college, or the cost of a decent used car, or even the cost of a nice, all-inclusive family vacation. Thankfully, the result was only a minor injury to my wife's hand and no lasting financial damage.

However, how many people get into a car accident or encounter some other medical emergency without health insurance? If an emergency room visit with an X-ray and stitches costs $4,000, imagine what a broken leg might cost; or an overnight stay in the hospital; or a minor procedure or operation, let alone a major one. Depending on the severity of a person's medical circumstances, inadequate, or no health insurance at all, could have that person owing thousands to tens of thousands, even hundreds of thousands of dollars.

As will be discussed in Chapter 10, one should not be naïve; oftentimes, medical bills are like any other form of credit: compounding interest is applied to the principal, or the amount of money you owe. Consequently, without adequate health insurance, you could be paying a medical bill for years, if not decades to come.

As will be discussed in Chapter 5, it is important to understand that you are your biggest asset. Therefore, first and foremost, you must take care of, and protect yourself. Along with eating a healthy diet, exercising regularly, and not smoking, having health insurance is a key component. Not having adequate health insurance exposes you to falling into serious debt in the unfortunate event that you need immediate medical attention.

Therefore, if you currently do not have adequate health insurance, it is imperative that you immediately investigate health insurance options for yourself and your family. By buying health insurance, you wisely transfer the risk and liability to someone else.

Speak with your current employer, and if you have an employed significant other, have them talk to their employer to see about health insurance options. Also, seek out health insurance options directly from hospitals and other health care providers in your area. Finally, depending on the country, state, county, and even city, seek out government-funded health insurance options. Many states in the U.S. offer some form of assistance to individuals and families who have certain income levels.

The bottom line is to begin to investigate your options and then choose one as soon as you can. Not only could it be the difference between life and death but it could also be the difference between thriving financially and going bankrupt.

LIFE INSURANCE

If you are your biggest asset, then your loved ones are your most precious possessions. It is therefore important to protect and provide for them in the unfortunate reality of you passing away, especially prematurely. Since tomorrow is promised to no one, it is imperative to plan for your family's tomorrow today. Thus, I highly recommend doing your own research and then speaking with an insurance expert to learn more about the various types of life insurance policies, including term, whole, and universal life insurance.

HOME AND AUTO INSURANCE

Two important things to keep in mind about home and auto insurance are the deductible and the liability amounts. The deductible is applied every time you file a claim. For example, if you get into a fender bender and your deductible is $500 and the damage done is $2,000, then you will have to pay the first $500 and your insurance will pay the remaining $1,500. Having a lower deductible usually means paying a higher premium, or the amount you pay for an insurance policy. Insurance companies want to recoup their possible losses from your lower deductible by making you pay more for your premium. Conversely, if you raise your deductible, then your premium will often be lower.

Auto liability insurance is a type of car insurance coverage that is required by law in most states. If you cause an accident, liability coverage helps pay for the other person's expenses. There are two types of auto liability coverage: bodily injury liability coverage, and property damage liability coverage.

If you are found to be at fault in an accident that injures another person, bodily injury liability coverage helps pay for that person's medical expenses. If you cause an accident that damages someone else's property (e.g., their car), property damage liability coverage pays for their repairs. You will also need to investigate collision, uninsured motorist, and other types of coverage in order to have the right auto insurance policy in place to protect you, your family, and your assets.

Therefore, once again, speak with an insurance expert about your individual needs and wishes to find out what would be the best home and auto insurance coverage for you. For example, I called my home and auto insurance agent and asked for various scenarios based on increasing or lowering my deductible and increasing or lowering my liability. By doing so, I found that if I doubled the deductible of my homeowners insurance, I would be able to double the liability coverage for about the same price as I was paying before with a lower deductible and half the liability. Once again, a higher deductible usually means lower premiums, which can then be used to increase your liability coverage to protect you and your assets even more.

Since potential damage while driving is much higher than potential damage to your home, auto insurance is usually much more expensive than homeowners insurance. Therefore, once again, I strongly urge you to speak with an insurance expert regarding how the different scenarios of increasing or lowering your deductible and increasing or lowering your liability could affect the cost of your premium and the type and amount of liability coverage you have. The hour or so you spend on the phone with your insurance provider going over the different scenarios is well worth your time and energy and should be made a priority.

RENTERS INSURANCE

A renters or tenant insurance policy is designed to help protect renters and their belongings. A typical policy includes liability coverage, protection for your belongings, and coverage for additional living expenses, should the home you are renting become temporarily uninhabitable. While you may not always be able to prevent certain situations, such as a break-in, a visitor's injury, or a fire in the unit next to yours that causes damage to your unit, renters or tenant insurance can help minimize the impact of these types of events.

If you do rent, speaking with an insurance agent could save you thousands, and perhaps even tens of thousands of dollars. Once again, it is important to remember the primary function of all types of insurance: insurance allows you to transfer your risk and your liability to someone else.

Having health, life, home or renters, and auto insurance is the number one most important thing you can do right now to protect yourself, your loved ones, and your assets. Without the right type and amount of insurance, you open yourself up to years, even decades of perpetual debt. Therefore, as I discuss in Chapter 3, it is best to be wise and get proper insurance immediately.

CHAPTER 3: THE DEBT MATRIX

THE MATRIX

The Matrix is a movie about a world where humans and computers are at war. Due to the use of nuclear weapons, the earth has been devastated, and the sky scorched in the hope of blocking the sun's rays, which serve as the energy source for the computers, thus hoping to stop the computers. However, in retaliation, the computers design an elaborate process of "growing" humans in order to harvest their thermal energy, which can be used to fuel their operating systems. In this post-apocalyptic world, most of the human race is born and bred by the computers in a suspended, alternate reality called "the Matrix."

The Matrix is a computer program where people live out their entire lives never knowing the difference between the Matrix and reality. As Morpheus, played by Laurence Fishburne, states, "The Matrix is the world that has been pulled over people's eyes to blind them from the truth." The Matrix is thus a prison for people's minds, and for most humans, the Matrix is their only reality. Neo, played by Keanu Reeves, was one such human.

While plugged into the Matrix, Neo senses something isn't right. It is something like a scratch he can't itch. Meanwhile, a group of humans, known as Zionists, have escaped the Matrix to fight the computers from both inside the Matrix and from the outside—in the real world. While observing the Matrix from the computers on his battleship, Morpheus, a Zionist commander, senses something special in Neo. Morpheus believes Neo to be "the One"—the one person who can defeat the computers from both inside and outside the Matrix. Therefore, Morpheus plugs into the Matrix in order to help release Neo's mind from the Matrix prison.

While plugged into the Matrix, Morpheus attempts to explain to Neo why he senses something is just not right. Morpheus offers Neo two choices in the form of two pills: a blue pill, and a red pill. Morpheus explains that the blue pill will knock Neo out and erase all memory of their meeting. By taking this pill, Neo can return to the suspended, plugged-in version of himself and live out the rest of his somewhat comfortable life as a prisoner in the alternate reality of the Matrix. However, the red pill will send Neo "down the rabbit hole" and jettison him from the Matrix to be reborn into a new world that sits outside of the Matrix, a world Neo was meant to live in, but one he has never known: the real world. Neo has critical a choice to make. Neo chooses the red pill.

The definition of "neo" is a new or revived form. Therefore, when Neo is unplugged from the Matrix and "reborn," he awakens in a computer-created, uterus-like cocoon, submerged in an embryonic-type fluid. Similar to a newborn baby, he has no body hair and is unable to use his muscles and eyes properly. Neo's real life has truly just begun. Being awakened to this new reality, Neo now sees the world through a very different lens. He begins his learning and training in order to fulfill the plans and purpose of his life as the One.

The Matrix was a system designed to keep the human race docile and in bondage so that the computers can harvest their thermal energy. The Matrix was a perfectly designed system to get the results needed by the computers. However, with the help of Morpheus and the other Zionists, by being freed from the Matrix, Neo affected the new reality by eventually defeating the computers. Neo "became the change he wanted to see in the world"—as Mahatma Gandhi once professed—by freeing people's minds.

DRAWING PARALLELS

Similar to the movie, *The Matrix*, how many people have consciously or subconsciously accepted their current financial reality as reality? Not thinking, believing, or understanding that a different reality can and does exist? A reality waiting to be discovered, awakened, and actualized. How many people are plugged into the debt matrix, living and operating in a "system" perfectly designed to get the results it gets? How many people are living in financial bondage that is caused by excessive debt?

Think about your current financial reality. What "systems" do you have in place that have produced the results you have gotten? For example, if you are in excessive debt, how did your "systems" of spending and decision-making lead you to your current financial reality? With this initial question in mind, it is important to reflect on the following questions in order to better understand your current "systems" of spending and decision-making.

- Do you have and follow a budget—a game plan—for your money? Or, do you just spend money, living day to day or month to month?

- Do you delay gratification and save money to buy things, or even go without, if you do not have the money? Or, do you buy things on credit whenever you want something?

- Do you buy things you can afford? Or, do you buy things even if you can only afford the minimum monthly payment to own those things?

- Do you save money for emergencies? Or, do you constantly accrue late fees and overdraft penalties from deficit spending when emergencies arise?

- Do you have financial goals that will allow you to be debt free, travel and take vacations, own a home, and invest for your future? Or, are you just living for the moment?

- Do you live within your means? Or, do you feel like you "deserve" more than you have, so you end up spending more than you have?

- Do you feel secure in who you are as a person? Or, do you consciously or subconsciously believe that acquiring "things" will make you happy and content?

Looking yourself in the mirror and answering these questions honestly is the first step in becoming a Neo in your own financial life. It is the first step to unplugging from the debt matrix. Although these questions are difficult, they are not meant to condemn you. Rather, they are intended to get at the core of the financial "systems" you have created for yourself.

Remember, right thinking is the raw material for right actions. People's actions will naturally reveal the direction of their thoughts. Therefore, if you want to redesign the reality of your finances, you have to begin to change how you see yourself and your finances.

By freeing people's minds from the Matrix, Neo became the change he wanted to see in the world. If you want to reach your financial goals of being debt free, traveling and taking vacations, owning a home, and investing for your future, then you must redesign your current financial reality with these goals in mind.

To have these goals become a reality, one must become a Neo in the financial matrix. One must not accept a current financial reality as the ultimate, locked-in reality. Know that there are more possibilities out there. And although it may be challenging in the beginning, it is necessary to realize that a different, and more importantly, a better reality exists. However, you will never know this unless you are willing to take the red pill and subject yourself to the possibilities of that new reality.

WISDOM AND INSANITY

Wisdom is difficult to define, but people usually recognize it when they hear it. Mostly, wisdom is related to the decision-making process. A definition of what psychologists view as wisdom involves the integration of knowledge, experience, and deep understanding that incorporates tolerance for the uncertainties of life. As a result, wise people generally share an optimism that life's problems can be solved. Because of this, they experience a certain amount of calm when facing difficult decisions.

Simply put, then, through knowledge, experience, and deep understanding, wisdom is the ability to face life's uncertainties with calm optimism. Wisdom emerges when people can learn from their past (or other people's pasts), allowing them to make better decisions in the future. With this explanation of wisdom as a backdrop, part of the process of becoming wiser in your financial life is addressing the insanity in your spending.

One definition of insanity is doing the same thing over and over and expecting different results. Thus, if the results from your current systems of spending are not desirable, then it is time to look at your systems. Just as this definition of insanity implies, you cannot keep spending money the way you always have and expect things to be different, let alone, better. With this in mind, I recommend the following in order for you to see all the different ways you are spending your money, how much you are spending, and why you are making those choices.

First, whether on a computer or in a journal, for a month or two, write down every dollar you spend.

Second, identify each expense or purchase as something you *needed*, something you *wanted*, or something you felt you *deserved*.

Third, if the expense or purchase was something you *wanted* or felt you *deserved*, if you are comfortable doing so, through honest reflection, write down what personal need the purchase was fulfilling. For example, if you spent $50 on a new pair of pants you *wanted*, you may write, "I wanted the pants because I was going out on a second date and wanted to look good."

Date	Expense or Purchase	Cost	Needed, wanted, or deserved	Personal need the purchase was attempting to fulfill

By writing down all of your expenses over a one- or two-month period, you will have a much clearer picture of where all your money is going. Furthermore, if done through honest reflection, you may even gain insight as to *why* you spend your money the way you do. Once this *why* comes into sharper focus (through knowledge, experience, and deeper understanding), you will be better equipped to make wiser money decisions in the future.

FILLING THE VOID

Unfortunately, I believe the overwhelming majority of people in the world have a void in their life. People try to fill this void in a myriad of ways: with the newest styles and latest gadgets; with job promotions and pay increases; with new cars, homes, and even spouses; with drugs, alcohol, and sex; with getting the most "likes" or followers on social media; with thrill-seeking; with overeating; and with religion, to name just a few. This void can also be connected to *why* people spend money the way they do.

Often, people's money is diverted to such activities and material things to fill the void. Yet, it is important to realize that although spending money in this way may bring short-term relief, it will never be a long-term solution. This is true because no matter where we go, there we are. These things will not bring us lasting happiness and contentment. Wearing expensive clothes, driving a new car, or eating at the best restaurants will not fill the deeper void.

What I have found is that all good things are gained in the long haul. Fulfilling things that bring real contentment usually take a large investment of time, energy, and priority to yield their positive results. Relationships, health, spirituality, wisdom, and, yes—even finances—have no quick fixes. If such quick fixes existed, then the world would be filled with far stronger marriages and relationships, as well as healthier and happier people who are financially viable.

The world today does not align with this long-haul perspective. If an Internet search does not yield a response within seconds, we automatically hit refresh. If a relationship gets rocky, we abandon it and find another one. If we have mental or physical ailments, we take a pill. If we are not "growing" spiritually, we look for another place or form of worship or religion. And, if we want or feel like we deserve something, we buy it immediately on credit and have it delivered overnight from halfway around the world.

I think a lot of people compare their Monday-through-Friday lives with other people's highlight reels. I know I did for a long time. As is well known, people often portray themselves in a very positive light on social media—taking selfies of themselves in beautiful places, having the times of their lives, and not portraying the struggles most people face on a daily basis. Actually, if someone did post their daily struggles and setbacks, eventually, many would probably "unfriend" them. It seems that being "real" is becoming a rare commodity.

The problem with this is that whenever we read or hear about a successful person, we only hear of their triumphs, not of the arduous journey riddled with various setbacks as they worked hard to reach a level of success. For example, you never hear about Thomas Edison's 1,000 plus failed attempts to invent the light bulb. Instead, we are left to marvel at how someone could have created such an innovative, ground-breaking, and world-changing invention. As will be discussed in Chapters 6 and 7, grit and having a growth mindset is what helped Edison invent the light bulb, not pure intellect.

The same could be said about my story, as well as your own. Some people reading this book might conclude: "Must be nice to have a college degree, work in the education profession, and have a good income with ample time off." However, what people could not know was how practically every winter and summer I got strep throat because of the stress of going to college, working, and trying to raise a family. My body would simply collapse at the end of each semester. Nor would people know the myriad other ways my wife and I struggled, sacrificed, and persevered in order to be where we are today. As always, there is more to the story than what one sees from the outside.

Therefore, do not think you are better or worse off than someone else based on outside appearances. For example, just because someone drives a BMW does not mean they can afford it. In order to keep up appearances, many people buy things based on paying the minimum payment that fits into their monthly budget, and not whether they can truly afford it. These individuals falsely compare their Monday-through-Friday lives with other people's highlight reels. Consequently, they are constantly coming up short, and look for the next thing to fill the void they feel.

As Chapter 4 will discuss, the unfortunate reality is that a majority of people have experienced some type of trauma in their lives. Trauma can both widen and deepen the void. Some people's reasons as to *why* they spend their money the ways they do may require counseling from professional mental health providers. With this reality in mind, this book will not provide quick fixes for your finances.

A case in point: many quick-fix diets work in the short term, but if eating healthy and exercising regularly does not become integrated into a person's lifestyle, the diet has little chance of working in the long run, and can even do more harm than good. Therefore, the goal of this book is to both assist you in understanding *why* you spend your money the way you do and to provide you with some suggestions and different ways of thinking in order to become wiser in *how* you spend your money. By understanding your past money choices, you can begin to unplug from the debt matrix and redesign the reality of your finances, forever.

CHAPTER 4: UNDERSTANDING THE WHY

ONE OF THE GREATEST FALLACIES

"Sticks and stones may break my bones, but words will never hurt me." If only that were true. If it were, then there would be so many more healthy, happy, and whole people on earth. Although words do not break bones, they do have the power to break promises, dreams, hearts, and spirits.

You will never hear a small child say, "I cannot wait until I get to high school so I can be lazy and unmotivated, fail most of my classes, and eventually drop out." After 22 years in public education and hundreds of interactions with students and their families, one belief that has become foundational in my view of young people is this: they all want to achieve and be successful, but for those who are not, something has prevented them from those goals.

For example, for the student who is deemed apathetic, there is a reason at the root of their apathy. For the student who is considered defiant, there is a reason at the root of their defiance. For the student who is labeled "at risk," there are reasons at the root of their academic and behavioral struggles. I know this may seem basic to many people, but my experience has been that oftentimes people will pursue the quick fix by dealing with the manifestations (i.e., the behaviors, whether they be apathetic, defiant, truant, substance abuse, or the like), and not take the time and energy to get at the root of *why* the manifestations or behaviors have occurred.

When speaking with a student who was struggling academically or behaviorally, I often equated their situation to someone whose diet consisted only of fast-food. I would explain that if a person were to eat only fast-food, after a while, he or she would begin to see weight gain, a loss of energy, and possibly an outbreak of acne. Basically, these outward signs are manifestations of things occurring on the inside.

Then, because of my foundational belief that all young people want to achieve and be successful, I make the connection of a poor diet and outward physical signs to the student's own current behaviors by proposing that his or her behaviors (i.e., apathetic, defiant, truant, substance abuse, etc.) are outward manifestations of what is going on inside. Unfortunately, I have had to use this analogy far too many times.

THE FOLLOWING IS ONE SUCH EXAMPLE

A high school sophomore was struggling both academically and behaviorally, so a student support team (SST) meeting was held to try to determine *why* this was the case. During the meeting, the student's behaviors were discussed, namely, their lack of effort, defiant attitude, and apathetic demeanor. After addressing the surface-level issues of attendance, grades, and conduct, the student was asked *why* she was struggling. Having already struggled through her first year of high school, she responded indifferently to the root question by giving one of the most popular student responses to the question of "*why*" by mumbling, "I don't know."

After the same question was asked several more times in different ways, each eliciting the same "I don't know" response, it was clear the student was done with the meeting. Unfortunately, like the majority of students who are called into such meetings, the only guardian in attendance was the mother. This is an unfortunate and all-too-common reality, since single mothers are the head-of-household in approximately 80 percent of single-parent homes.

During the entire meeting, I wanted to ask a tough question. When I saw she was not going to provide us with much information, I decided to ask it gently: "I notice your dad is not here. Where is he?" Immediately upon asking, her eyes began to tear up as she tried desperately to hold back the tears. Seeing her daughter begin to cry, the mother informed us that her father had been battling cancer for the past two years and was currently at home, unable to get out of bed. Instantly, my mind went to what it must be like for this young woman, seeing her once strong, vibrant dad slowly withering away, too weak to get out of bed, to say nothing of the nights of hearing him groan in pain.

After hearing about her home life, the reason for her apathy and defiant behavior became crystal clear. Although the information and situation did not excuse her behavior, it did provide valuable insights as to *why* she was performing and behaving the way she was. Therefore, in order to assist her with the emotional toll of seeing her dad struggle with cancer, we set her up with one of the school therapists. Additionally, after asking for her and her mother's consent, we notified her teachers of the situation so that they would be aware and make any appropriate accommodations for her should the need arise.

Unless people are willing to take the time and energy to understand the *why* by asking difficult, trauma-informed questions, attributing students who struggle academically or behaviorally to a matter of simply being apathetic or defiant is just as convenient as saying that people who are obese are lazy. There are underlying causes to many, if not most, negative manifestations.

ADVERSE CHILDHOOD EXPERIENCES (ACES)

The following overview on adverse childhood experiences (ACEs) comes from acestoohigh.com.

In 1985, Dr. Vincent Felitti, a physician and chief of Kaiser

Permanente's Department of Preventive Medicine, could not figure out why each year, for the prior five years, more than half of the people in his obesity clinic had dropped out—a clinic designed for people who were 100 to 600 pounds overweight. What was even more perplexing for Felitti was that all of the people who had dropped out had actually been losing weight.

Some people were 300 pounds overweight, but lost 100 pounds, and then chose to drop out. Wanting to understand *why*, Felitti began to dig into these people's medical records. He found several startling similarities: 1) all dropouts had been born at a normal weight; 2) they did not gain weight slowly over several years, but rather, their weight gain happened abruptly; and 3) if they lost weight, they would regain all of it—or even more—in a very short period of time.

Yet, these similarities still did not answer *why* people were dropping out, so Felitti decided to conduct face-to-face interviews with several hundred of those who had left the program. The turning point in Felitti's quest came about by accident. During the interviews, Felitti asked a battery of questions, including, "How much did you weigh when you were born?" and "How much did you weigh when you entered high school?"

During these question-and-answer sessions, Felitti once misspoke and asked one patient, "How much did you weigh when you were first sexually active?" The female patient responded, "Forty pounds." Not understanding what he was hearing, Felitti asked the exact same question again. Again, the woman gave the same answer, but this time she burst into tears and added, "It was when I was four years old. With my father." Querying the other patients, Felitti saw a disturbing pattern: every other person was providing information about childhood sexual abuse.

Worried that he was injecting some unconscious bias, Felitti asked several of his colleagues to interview the next 100 patients in the weight program. The results they found were the same: of the 286 highly obese people interviewed, most had been sexually abused as children. As startling as this was, it turned out to be less significant than another piece of information that dropped into place during an interview with a particular woman who had been raped when she was 23 years old. In the year after the attack, she told Felitti she had gained 105 pounds. "As she was thanking me for asking the question," says Felitti, "she looked down at the carpet, and muttered, 'Overweight is overlooked, and that's the way I need to be.'" Through this encounter, Felitti realized that many extremely obese people didn't see their weight as a problem, but rather, as a solution. Similar to alcohol, tobacco, or illegal drugs, eating soothed their anxiety, fear, anger, or depression. For this woman, being obese protected her because it made her invisible to men.

This realization provides more understanding as to *why* millions of people around the world use biochemical coping methods (i.e., alcohol, marijuana, food, sex, tobacco, violence, thrill sports, and more) to escape intense anxiety, fear, anger, or depression. Even though many of these methods may have negative consequences, for many people, such methods provide a temporary, but gratifying solution.

Needing to expand his study beyond the subset of several hundred of people in the obesity program, Dr. Felitti joined with Dr. Robert Anda and asked 26,000 San Diego Kaiser Permanente members if they would be interested in helping them understand how childhood events might affect adult health. Of the 26,000 members, 17,421 agreed to participate in their study. The doctors spent a year researching childhood trauma, specifically focusing on the major types of trauma that many of the patients had mentioned in Felitti's original research. Below are the 10 ACEs the researchers measured:

> Physical, sexual, and verbal abuse

Physical and emotional neglect

A family member who is:
- depressed or diagnosed with other mental illnesses
- addicted to alcohol or other substances
- in prison

Witness to a mother being abused

Losing a parent to separation, divorce, or another reason

Each type of ACE counted as one point, no matter how many times that one experience occurred. For example, a person experiencing verbal abuse by living with an alcoholic father and a mentally ill mother would have an ACEs score of three. Seventy-five percent of the 17,421 participants were White, 11 percent Latino, 7.5 percent Asian and Pacific Islander, and 5 percent were Black. They were middle-class (they were able to afford Kaiser Medical Insurance) and middle-aged (their average age was 57). Additionally, 36 percent had attended at least some college, and 40 percent had college degrees or higher. Upon seeing the results, Dr. Anda said, "I wept. I saw how much people had suffered and I wept."

The conclusions drawn from the ACEs study found that the greater the number of ACEs, the greater the risk for an array of poor physical, mental, and behavioral health outcomes for patients across their life spans. As Wolpow (2016) shares,

> In scientific terms, there was a direct "dose-response" relationship between adverse childhood experiences and serious health issues. We cannot draw a straight line between ACEs and outcomes. However, we do know that the higher the ACEs score in

a given population, the greater the probabilities of the following co-occurring conditions:

Alcoholism and alcohol abuse; chronic obstructive pulmonary disease and ischemic heart disease; depression; fetal death; high risk sexual behavior; illicit drug use; intimate partner violence; liver disease; obesity; sexually transmitted disease; smoking; suicide attempts; and unintended pregnancy. (p. 5)

Unfortunately, about two-thirds of the adults in the study had experienced at least one type of ACE. And of those, 87 percent had experienced two or more types, showing that ACEs usually did not happen in isolation (i.e., an alcoholic family member could have also been verbally or physically abusive).

Things got very serious when a person's ACEs score was four or more. Compared to people with an ACEs score of zero, those with four had a 240 percent greater risk of hepatitis, were 390 percent more likely to have chronic obstructive pulmonary disease (i.e., emphysema or chronic bronchitis), and a 240 percent higher risk of contracting a sexually transmitted disease. They were also twice as likely to be smokers, 12 times more likely to have attempted suicide, 7 times more likely to be an alcoholic, and 10 times more likely to have injected street drugs. Overall, approximately 22 percent of the participants had an ACEs score of three, and about 13 percent had a score of four or more. People with an ACEs score of 6 or higher were at risk of their life span being shortened by 20 years.

EFFECTS OF ACES

In conjunction with the ACEs research, other, parallel studies have been published linking how something that happened to a person when they were a child can land them in the hospital as an adult. For example, the stress of severe, chronic childhood trauma, such as being regularly hit, constantly being belittled and berated, or watching a father regularly hit one's mother, releases hormones that physically damage a child's developing brain.

As shared on acestoohigh.com, pediatrician Nadine Burke Harris explains that if a person is in a forest and sees a bear, a very efficient fight or flight system instantly floods their body with adrenaline and cortisol and shuts off the thinking portion of the brain that would stop to consider other options. This, of course, is very helpful if you are in a forest and need to run from a bear. However, as Dr. Harris states, "The problem is when that bear comes home from the bar every night." In other words, the fight, flight, or freeze hormones can become toxic when they are turned on for too long.

Thus, if a "bear" threatens a child almost every single day, the child's emergency response system is activated over and over and over again. That child is always ready to fight or flee from the "bear," but the part of his or her brain that is called upon to diagram a sentence or do math—the prefrontal cortex—becomes stunted, because emergencies—such as fleeing bears—take precedence over doing math. Dr. Harris says of her patients who have had four or more categories of ACEs, "Their odds of having learning or behavior problems in school were 32 times as high as kids who had no adverse childhood experiences."

Again, according to acestoohigh.com, "Children with toxic stress live much of their lives in fight, flight or fright [freeze] mode. They respond to the world as a place of constant danger. With their brains overloaded with stress hormones and unable to function appropriately, they can't focus on learning. They fall behind in school or fail to develop healthy relationships with peers or create problems with teachers and principals because they are unable to trust adults. Some kids do all three. With despair, guilt and frustration pecking away at their psyches, they often find solace in food, alcohol, tobacco, methamphetamines, inappropriate sex, high-risk sports, and/or work or over-achievement. They don't regard these coping methods as problems. Consciously or unconsciously, they use them as solutions to escape from depression, anxiety, anger, fear, and shame. Children affected by ACEs appear in all human service systems throughout the lifespan—childhood, adolescence, and adulthood—as clients with behavioral, learning, social, criminal, and chronic health problems."

ACES SURVEY QUESTIONS

The following questionnaire comes from acestoohigh.com.

Answer "YES" or "NO" to each of the ten questions:

While you were growing up, during your first 18 years of life:

- Did a parent or other adult in the household often swear at you, put you down, or humiliate you? Or, act in a way that made you afraid that you might be physically hurt?

- Did a parent or other adult in the household often push, grab, slap, or throw something at you? Or, ever hit you so hard that you had marks or were injured?

- Did an adult or person at least five years older than you ever touch or fondle you or have you touch their body in a sexual way? Or, try to actually have anal, oral, or vaginal sex with you?

- Did you often feel that no one in your family loved you or thought you were important or special? Or, your family didn't look out for each other, feel close to each other, or support each other?

- Did you often feel that you didn't have enough to eat, had to wear dirty clothes, and had no one to protect you? Or, your parents were too drunk or high to take care of you or take you to the doctor if you needed it?

• Were your parents ever separated or divorced?

• Was your mother or stepmother often pushed, grabbed, slapped, or had something thrown at her? Or, sometimes or often kicked, bitten, hit with a fist, or hit with something hard? Or, ever repeatedly hit for at least a few minutes or threatened with a gun or a knife?

• Did you live with anyone who was a problem drinker or alcoholic or who used street drugs?

• Was a household member depressed or mentally ill or did a household member attempt suicide?

• Did a household member go to prison?

Add up your "YES" answers. Your "YES" answers would be your ACEs score (0 to 10 ACEs)

UNDERSTANDING THE *WHY*

Just like the struggling sophomore discussed at the beginning of the chapter who, day by day, witnessed her father dying of cancer, are there manifestations of your past or current trauma or pain that can be seen in your current systems of spending money? Through honest reflection, it is important to ask whether you spend a considerable amount of money on biochemical coping methods, such as alcohol, marijuana, food, sex, tobacco, or thrill sports, to escape intense anxiety, fear, anger, or depression. Or do you try to fill the void in your life by living beyond your means, like buying things you cannot afford in the hopes of addressing the unfulfilled needs in your life? Or do you simply just spend money in the moment without really thinking of, or fully understanding, the consequences of those actions on your future?

Lastly, consider this: for most purchases people make that they cannot really afford, the *what*, the *where*, and the *when* of such purchases are oftentimes manifestations of the *why* they are choosing to make those purchases. Therefore, a major first step in redesigning the reality of your finances and becoming the best, healthiest version of yourself in all aspects of your life is taking a hard look in the mirror to try to understand *why* you do what you do. This very much includes attempting to understand *why* you spend your money the way you do. Here, seeking out a trained and trusted counselor or therapist who can assist you in walking through and working out your past traumas or pains in order to redesign your future may well be worth the time, energy, and money.

Recall the direct "dose-response" relationship between ACEs and serious health issues. Although researchers cannot draw a straight line between ACEs and behavioral outcomes, they do know that the higher the ACEs score in a given population, the greater the *probability* that those people will be affected with behavioral, learning, social, criminal, and chronic health problems throughout their lives. However, please note the word *"probabilities."* If you have experienced numerous ACEs, please know that you are not a statistic, and thus, it is not preordained that you will live a more difficult life.

To bring this point home, I do trauma-informed care training for schools. Part of this training is having teachers, staff members, and administrators take the ACEs questionnaire. My goal in doing so is to demonstrate to educators how pervasive trauma is in society, even among their own colleagues. Out of 213 respondents who were willing to share the results of their ACEs survey, 76 percent had experienced at least one or more ACEs, 29 percent had experienced four or more ACEs, and 17 percent had experienced six or more ACEs. What is important to keep in mind is that many, if not all, of the 213 respondents had gone on to graduate from college, and some of those had even earned advanced degrees.

Therefore, there is hope. People get counseling. People get help. People are resilient. People have grit. People overcome. People change. People grow. People thrive. Taking care of yourself so that you can become the best, healthiest version of yourself must become one of your top priorities because you are your and your family's biggest asset.

CHAPTER 5: YOUR BIGGEST ASSET: YOU

LOVE DOES

Although people reading this book are vastly different, one constant is this: you are your biggest asset. If you are not the best, healthiest version of yourself, no amount of money is going to make you happy. So, although this book is about your finances, be sure to invest the proper amount of time, energy, and priority in focusing on your physical, mental, emotional, spiritual, and social needs. Remembering that there are no quick fixes; attending to these needs will require action and probably a change of attitude, perspective, and mindset. However, as expressed most powerfully in the title of Bob Goff's 2014 book, *Love Does*, action is the key.

Besides being an author, Goff is also a lawyer, and he opens his book *Love Does* by describing one of the places he goes to work and think: Tom Sawyer Island at Disneyland. As he explains, Tom Sawyer Island was a source of one of Goff's epiphanies:

> Here's a strange truth I've noticed. Almost everyone knows about Tom Sawyer Island at Disneyland, but most people don't go. Maybe it's because it's surrounded by water and you have to take a raft to get there. But that's not that tough to do. Lots of people *want* to go. Some people even plan to go. But most forget or just don't get around to it. It's one of those "we'll do that next trip" kinds of places for a lot of people. Tom Sawyer

Island is like most people's lives, I think: they never get around to crossing over to it.

Living a life fully engaged and full of whimsy and the kind of things that love does is something most people plan to do, but along the way they just kind of forgot. Their dreams become one of those "we'll go there next time" deferrals. The sad thing is, for many there is no "next time" because passing on the chance to cross over is an overall attitude toward life rather than a single decision. They need a change of attitude, not more opportunities.

As I sit on my [Tom Sawyer] island, it becomes clear that we need to stop plotting the course and instead just land the plane on our plans to make a difference by getting to the "do" part of faith. That's because love is never stationary. In the end, love doesn't just keep thinking about it or keep planning for it. Simply put: love does. (pp. xii-xiv)

What do you need to do to redesign your current reality? What course of action have you been plotting for days, weeks, months, years, or even decades that you have yet to act on? What dreams of yours are slowly becoming a "we'll go there next time" deferral? How is your current attitude affecting your current reality? The bottom line is that if you are not happy with where you are in your life, then you must first look inside yourself for the answers. It all begins with you. As Mahatma Gandhi professed, "Become the change that you wish to see in the world."

As it relates to your finances, it will be crucial to invest in yourself by investing in your education. Your education is the best financial investment you can make. However, like all good things, your education is a long-haul commitment. I firmly believe it is never too late to go back to school. Yes, it will be difficult to return to your education while raising children, working a day job, or scraping by while you attend. However, the benefits, both personally and financially, will, over time, far outweigh the difficulties.

I used to work with a woman who became a high school librarian by taking one or two college classes each semester. While raising children, it took her over eight years to graduate. Talk about a long-haul investment. In another case, while being an adult school administrator, I witnessed a retired military veteran who was in his late seventies return to his studies to get his general equivalency diploma (GED); he had promised his late wife that he would graduate high school one day. If they can do it, so can you.

A DIFFICULT REALITY

According to the National Center for Education Statistics, in 2012, the percentage of high school dropouts among persons 16 through 24 years old was 6.6 percent, with Whites, Blacks, and Hispanics amounting to, respectively, 4.3 percent, 7.5 percent, and 12.7 percent of the total. As numerous studies have confirmed, life can be more difficult for high school dropouts because they are less likely to find jobs and earn good living wages. This, then, increases the probabilities that they will live in poverty, rely on public assistance, suffer from a variety of adverse health outcomes, and engage in crime (Rumberger, 2013).

Furthermore, Harrington (2017), quoting Rumberger shares, "The most vulnerable and disadvantaged populations in our country and many countries are those who are the least educated....They [the high school dropouts] die nine years sooner on average than high school graduates, earn half a million dollars less over their lifetimes, are five or six times more likely to be incarcerated, and tend to rank low in most indicators of well-being, including poverty" (pp. 4-5). In today's society, having a high school diploma is needed to get almost any kind of job in the U.S., and further education and training (often a college degree) are crucial to staying out of poverty.

Consequently, according to the Bureau of Labor Statistics, based on educational attainment, the 2014 median monthly earnings for full-time wage and salary workers age 25 and over were as follows:

Advanced degree:	$5,821
Bachelor's degree and higher:	$5,011
Bachelor's degree only:	$4,624
Some college or associate's degree:	$3,196
High school diploma, no college:	$2,806
Less than a high school diploma:	$2,050

(Note: I took the weekly averages and multiplied them by 4.2 to get the monthly averages.)

As one can see, generally speaking, the more education a person has, the more money they will make. Furthermore, although many can attest to the fact that money alone will not make you happy, it does provide more choices and opportunities, which can make life far easier to navigate. Based on this information, just by graduating from high school, a person will make approximately $756 per month more than a person who did not earn a high school diploma: $2,806 per month (with a high school diploma) – $2,050 per month (less than a high school diploma) = $756 per month.

Now, let's see this difference in income for a person who earns a high school diploma versus one who drops out of school before earning their diploma over time:

1 year	$9,072 ($756 x 12 months)
5 years	$45,360
10 years	$90,720
20 years	$181,440
30 years	$272,160

40 years	$362,880
50 years	$453,600

Just think, the above figures are simply the difference between a person who earns a high school diploma versus one who leaves school before earning one. Now, let's look at the difference between a person who graduates from college versus a person without a high school diploma:

$4,624 per month (bachelor's degree) − $2,050 per month (less than a high school diploma) = $2,574 per month.

1 year	$30,888 ($2,574 x 12 months)
5 years	$154,440
10 years	$308,880
20 years	$617,760
30 years	$926,664
40 years	$1,235,520
50 years	$1,544,440

Although these numbers are all averages and only approximates, the figures don't lie: investing in yourself by investing in your education is, indeed, a solid investment. Simply put, education is powerful.

EDUCATION AND INCOME: A VISUAL

When I worked in schools, and when I had the money on hand, I would withdraw $2,400 in one-dollar bills—24 stacks of one-dollar bills, with each stack totaling $100. I would use the money to demonstrate the difference between the monthly income of a high school dropout and that of a high school graduate. I would then do the same with the income of college students: those who attended and finished college compared to those who had dropped out of high school. The bank tellers hated when I made these withdrawals, but they also understood and appreciated what I was trying to do.

First, I would pull out eight stacks of bills and put them on the table. This amount, I would tell my students, was the difference in median monthly income between a high school dropout and a high school graduate: a high school graduate makes approximately $800 (rounding up from $756) more each month than a high school dropout. Then, I would ask them to think about what they could do with an extra $800 each month. Or, after dividing that amount by 30 days, what they could do with an extra $27 per day. In fact, this is quite a bit of money for a lot of people, let alone adolescents.

Next, I would pull out another eight stacks of bills and explain that this $1,600 was approximately how much more a person with some college, a trade (e.g., plumber), or a certified skill (e.g., dental assistant) could make each month over a person who had dropped out of high school. Finally, I would pull out the last eight stacks of bills—making a mound of money on the table—and explain that this $2,400 is approximately how much more per month a college graduate will make over a high school dropout.

Of course, I could just as easily have used stacks of green paper with one-dollar bills on the tops and bottoms. Regardless of how I did it, as you can imagine, this visual was a powerful one: more education = more money (earning potential); more money = more choices; more choices = more opportunities; more opportunities = broadening horizons and experiencing life in ways one never knew existed.

POVERTY AND THE ACHIEVEMENT GAP

The power and importance of education are not only isolated to one's earning potential. Keeping in mind the relationship between education and earning potential, the information below demonstrates how a student's household income and the education levels of their parents or guardians can directly affect that student's academic achievement on state standardized tests.

Based on California Department of Education data, the following information provides the percentages of California students who either met or exceeded standards on the California Assessment of Student Performance and Progress (CAASPP), English Language Arts (ELA), and Mathematics tests in the 2015–16 school year.

Pertaining to household income (economically disadvantaged—low income—versus not economically disadvantaged), the data revealed that from the 3rd grade to the 11th grade, there was an approximate 24 to 35 percentage-point difference in the number of students meeting or exceeding the standards on the ELA portion of the CAASPP, and a 27 to 37 percentage-point difference in the number of students meeting or exceeding the standards on the mathematics portion of the CAASPP. Basically, students from more affluent homes performed much better than their peers coming from impoverished homes.

Pertaining to parent and guardian education levels, the data revealed that from the 3rd grade to the 11th grade, the difference between a student whose parent or guardian did not have a high school diploma compared to a student whose parent or guardian had a high school diploma was a 7 to 10 percentage-point difference in either meeting or exceeding the standards on the ELA portion of the CAASPP, and a 3 to 7 percentage-point difference in either meeting or exceeding the standards on the mathematics portion of the CAASPP.

However, the difference between a student whose parent or guardian did not have a high school diploma compared to one whose parent or guardian was a college graduate was a 29 to 40 percentage-point difference on meeting or exceeding the standards on the ELA portion of the CAASPP, and 31 to 38 percentage-point difference on meeting or exceeding the standards on the mathematics portion of the CAASPP. This signifies that students from homes where a parent or guardian was a college graduate performed much better than their peers coming from homes where parents or guardians had not graduated from high school.

Unfortunately, this California trend of economically disadvantaged students performing lower on state standardized tests is not uncommon. Actually, they are the norm. After studying the income achievement gap in the United States over the last five decades, Reardon (2013, as cited by Silvernail, Sloan, Paul, Johnson, & Stump, 2014) concludes, "If we do not find ways to reduce the growing inequality in education outcomes—between the rich and the poor—schools will no longer be the great equalizer we want them to be" (p. 1). This income achievement gap is real; research and data bear witness to it. However, scoring lower on state standardized tests is not the only effect of this gap.

To better understand the effects of poverty and the income achievement gap on students, a synopsis of research findings has been compiled by the Tauck Family Foundation (2013, as cited by Silvernail, Sloan, Paul, Johnson, & Stump, 2014, pp. 2–3). The Tauck Family Foundation reported that researchers have found:

- Children from low-income households entering kindergarten and the first grade are already significantly behind their more affluent peers in terms of both academic knowledge and cognitive and social skills.

- Third-graders who both live in poverty and read below grade level are three times more likely to drop out of high school than students who have never been poor.

- Fourth-graders from low-income families are likely to be three years academically behind their peers from affluent families.

- Sixth-graders in high-poverty schools who fail at either math or English or who receive an unsatisfactory behavior grade have a 75 percent chance of dropping out of high school.

- Students in low-performing schools are five times more likely to drop out of high school than their peers from high-performing schools.

- High school seniors from low-income families are, on average, four years behind their higher-income peers.

- Only one out of two students from low-income families graduate high school.

- Nationally, only 33 percent of high school students from low-income households go to college, and only 8 percent will complete a degree within six years of matriculation.

Unfortunately, the previously presented California CAASPP data bears witness to these national trends. As one can see, the disparity between students who are economically disadvantaged compared to those who are not is evident by the third grade. Sadly, for many, the disparity then persists through the students' 12 years of schooling. They simply never catch up.

However, there is hope. If you come from or are currently living in poverty, you can become the change that you want to see in your family. Education is so powerful that it can change the trajectory of a person's life, for generations. By pursuing one's education, people can go to college and access career opportunities that, for many, break the cycle of poverty. They become role models for their children and their children's children, and this effect can continue for generations to come.

The following is one such example.

SUNDAY MORNING DEALS

With the sentence, "Give me whatever you have in your pocket," I sold my 1967 Ford Mustang to a student I had been mentoring. Unfortunately, this student, like many others, came from a very difficult background. Having both parents heavily into drugs and alcohol, he was practically left alone to raise himself. But he had thoroughly impressed me with his resilience, and this had made me want to help him be successful. It was clear to me that he was determined to make a better life for himself.

I will never forget the morning when I felt God impress upon me to sell this student my Mustang. Although the car was a classic, it was riddled with problems (more to come about the Mustang in Chapter 6). Regardless, the motor was strong and the car, for the most part, ran well. Being married, with two children, and barely making it on a beginning teacher's salary, I began to negotiate with God my car's selling price that Sunday morning. In my mind, I started by saying, "I'll give him a great deal and sell it for $1,500." Then, I felt God impress upon me a different answer, "It needs to be lower." Next, I bargained, "Okay, $1000." His response, "Nope. Lower." Again, I negotiated, "$750." Again, He said, "Lower." Me: "$500." Him: "Lower." Finally, my last plea: "$250?" Then, God gently responded, "Son, trust Me. Just give him the car." As I sat there, I realized what God was asking, and a deep peace engulfed me and tears began to stream down my face. Like so many times before that day, I knew God would provide.

Because of my heartfelt thankfulness for what God had afforded me, I felt compelled by love to give. Therefore, in order to make it a legal transaction, when I saw the student on Monday morning, I said,

"Give me whatever you have in your pocket, and the Mustang is yours." Being heavily into cars and enrolled in auto shop all four years of high school, the student was already a competent student-mechanic. Once the car was in his possession, he worked on it every day. During this time, I continued to speak with him and encouraged him to go after his dreams of being the first one in his family to graduate from college.

Eventually, he graduated from high school and joined the National Guard. While in the National Guard, I helped him enroll in community college and paid for some of his tuition and books. After one year in the service, he was deployed to Iraq, where he did two tours of duty. When he returned from the Middle East, he continued with his community college classes and finished his general education studies. He then transferred to, and graduated from, San Diego State University. The last time I spoke with him, he was married with two children, had just bought his first house, and was operating his own business. He broke the cycle of poverty and changed the trajectory of his and his family's life, likely for generations to come.

Since you are your biggest asset, if you have not already done so, be sure to invest in yourself by investing in your education. I have seen firsthand, through this young man and many others like him, all the rewards an education can bring.

CHAPTER 6: CHANGING TRAJECTORIES, FOR GENERATIONS

GRIT

In her 2013 TED Talk, *Grit: The Power of Passion and Perseverance*, later expanded and published as a book, Angela Lee Duckworth discusses the power of grit, or, as she defines it, "the passion and perseverance for very long-term goals." Duckworth was a seventh-grade math teacher when she first began to observe and question why some of her students did better than others. In her TED Talk, Duckworth states, "What struck me was that IQ was not the only difference between my best and my worst students. Some of my strongest students did not have stratospheric IQ scores, while some of my smartest kids weren't doing so well."

Duckworth continues by explaining, "After several more years in education, I came to the conclusion that what we need in education is a much better understanding of students and learning from a motivational perspective, from a psychological perspective. In education, the one thing we know how to measure best is IQ. But what if doing well in school and in life depends on much more than your ability to learn quickly and easily?"

Duckworth thus chose to go back to college and study psychology in order to determine what attributes, characteristics, or qualities make people successful. She began to study people in very challenging settings, and in every study she conducted, she asked the same question, "Who is successful here and why?" Duckworth and her research team studied cadets at West Point Military Academy, competitors in the National Spelling Bee, beginning teachers working in very tough neighborhoods, salespeople working for private companies, and thousands of high school students, all in order to try to determine who is, or would become successful and why.

After studying people in various challenging settings, Duckworth reports, "In all those very difficult contexts, one characteristic emerged as a significant predictor of success. And it wasn't social intelligence. It wasn't good looks, physical health, and it wasn't IQ. It was grit. Grit is passion and perseverance for very long-term goals. Grit is having stamina. Grit is sticking to your future, day in, day out, not just for the week, not just for the month, but for years, and working really hard to make that future a reality. Grit is like living life like a marathon, not a sprint."

As will be discussed in Chapter 7, Duckworth says that one of the best ways to develop grit is by developing a "growth mindset," or, the belief that through effort, people's abilities—including intelligence—can change and grow. We thus see that your current reality (including your current financial reality) can change with effort and grit.

GRIT PERSONIFIED

My college experience was not the norm. As I shared previously, my wife and I got married and had children at a very young age. Wanting to provide the best I could for my family, I decided to return to college and pursue my goal of becoming a social science teacher. Working three nights a week as a busboy and attending school full-time while also being a husband and father was difficult. However, if we allow them to, the difficult situations we traverse throughout our lives actually become the fabric of who we are, as they refine the innate qualities and characteristics that make us, well, us.

Whether good or bad, we can often look back after the fact and understand, and even sometimes be thankful for, the things we have gone through as we pursued our goals and dreams. As someone once told me, one can look at difficult and challenging times as a foundation for a great story to tell others later on, which can bring much bonding, gratitude, and even laughter. Of course, I'm not talking about life-threatening or abusive situations here, but lesser challenges. For example, my 1967 Ford Mustang is one of many sources of great laughter for my wife and I during this season of our lives, but only because we survived it.

My 1967 Ford Mustang was my friend. I would often speak to it, thanking it for taking such good care of me by being so reliable, even though it was slowly falling apart because I had no money nor skill to repair it. The reason I would periodically speak to my car was because the radio and tape player (yes, tape player...it was a long time ago) did not work. Not only did the radio not function, but the brakes would not engage until they were less than half an inch to the floor, forcing whoever was driving to pump them repeatedly in order to stop completely. Stopping on a dime was not a reality with this car.

Additionally, dangerously, the gas pedal would often stick to the floor, forcing the driver to place my foot under the pedal and kick it up. The car, by the way, was a three-speed manual stick shift, which led me to perform something of a dance routine between the gas, brake, and clutch pedals in order for it to both go and stop.

Making matters even worse was the fact that the ignition was worn, so that it was more like a hole than a fitted slot for the key. While driving, sometimes the key would actually fall out of the ignition. This may or may not have been a huge issue except for the fact that there was a one-inch-diameter, rusted-out hole in the floor of the car underneath the steering wheel. Although the key did fall out of the ignition on numerous occasions, I thanked God that it never fell through the rusted-out hole while driving.

Finally, and most humorously, was when one would turn the steering wheel and the horn would honk, and simultaneously—for no apparent reason—spark. Driving that car was always an adventure; so much so that my wife and I decided that whoever had the kids was not allowed to drive them in the Mustang. The Mustang had nothing "powered": no power brakes (obviously), or power windows, steering, or air-conditioning. It had an old-school, wood steering wheel with metal inlays, which would become blistering hot in the sun. When I drove it, I felt my hands burning because I had to grip the steering wheel very, very hard in order to turn—remember, it had no power steering.

What finally made me realize that I needed to find another car was when I went to park it one day, and the steering wheel came completely off the steering column. After this happened—and until I found another car—I had to carry a crescent wrench with me at all times in order to tighten the steering column bolt before I drove. This was clearly not a safe situation, but when you do not have a lot, sometimes you learn to endure a lot.

Being totally broke, my wife and I applied for Medi-Cal—California's state-funded insurance—and food stamps. Although it was not much, they did help, and I was thankful for having been able to receive this assistance. Yet, I did not want to remain in that situation, so I worked hard to complete college as quickly as I could, often taking five or six classes each semester. After four years—two years at a community college, and two years at San Diego State University (SDSU)—I graduated with my social science bachelor's degree. And though I graduated on a Thursday, I was back in school the following Monday so I could begin two summer school classes, which I needed to complete to be accepted into SDSU's teaching credential program.

Even with a wife and two children, attending college had been fairly easy once I figured out the "game" of college: creating proper systems to juggle the how, what, when, and where of studying. However, student teaching was a whole different ball game, and was the most stressful time of my life. The reason it was so stressful was because when I was placed at the school site for my student-teaching assignment, several teachers approached me and told me that one of my advisors (Ms. Jones, a teacher at the school) was "one of the best historians in the district. She will either make sure you get a job in the district or make sure that you do not." It put a lot of pressure on me to do well because my family was depending on me.

Student teaching, working, attending night classes for the teaching credential program, and preparing daily lesson plans, while also trying to be emotionally and physically present for my family, was eventually too much. Something had to give. Therefore, I decided to quit my job as a busboy and take out a student loan. By doing so, my wife and I forfeited our food stamps, and would not be able to qualify for them again until the money from the loan was gone. Finally, after a year of student teaching, I was rewarded with my teaching credential. With a little over $2,000 to our names—money left over from the student loan—I dove headfirst into the most difficult part of becoming a teacher: finding a job.

Having just turned twenty-six, having been married for six years, and having a six- and a three-year-old, I desperately sought and prayed for a teaching job. I applied to every and all types of schools in San Diego County: middle schools, high schools, and even military bases. After what felt like an eternity, one day, finally, I got a call for an interview.

As I entered the elevator that would take me to the interview, another candidate got on, and we went up together. The gentleman was in his late thirties and a veteran teacher who had been teaching in the deserts of Riverside County, but who was trying to get a job in the much-coveted San Diego area.

I truly do not believe he meant to be disrespectful or antagonistic by what he said to me on our elevator ride up. Rather, I honestly think he was just informing me of the way he thought it was. Essentially, he said, "No offense, but someone like you, fresh out of college, is never going to find a job in San Diego. There are too many veteran teachers like me with years of experience trying to come here. You may want to think about applying to districts in central or eastern California."

In the end, I did not get that job, but I was contacted several weeks later for an interview and was then offered a high school social science teaching position in the same district where I had been a student teacher. Not only was the position in San Diego it was also only a ten-minute drive from where we were living at the time. For five long years, my family and I had worked together to reach this goal. We had grit.

Although my first net paycheck as a teacher in 1996 was only $1,450 (teachers got paid once a month, ten months a year), it seemed like a fortune to me, especially since I was able to pay for health insurance for my family. And although grateful for the past support, we were no longer dependent on government assistance. Now, today, 27 years of marriage later, after surviving those tough early days, I look back with extreme gratitude for having lived through those years. Not only that, but often my family and I will reminisce about those days and just laugh at how absolutely crazy they were.

TIME AND MUSCLE

Whenever I hear people say, "I cannot afford to go to college or go back to school," my response is always, "You cannot afford not to." As discussed in Chapter 5, there is a direct relationship between education levels and income levels: the more education you have, the more money you make. Yes, there are people who have dropped out of high school and have become very successful financially. Yes, there are people who have earned advanced degrees and who still struggle financially. However, be careful not to make the exception the rule. Although there are always outliers—people who lie outside the expected range of statistical probability—the relationship between education and income hold true for most people.

The hard truth is that without a college degree, or some type of advanced training or certified trade or skill (e.g., training to become a plumber, mechanic, dental assistant, real estate agent, or electrician), the most people can offer an employer is their time and muscle. The unfortunate reality is that there are a lot of people with time and muscle, which is the reason why income levels are so much lower for people with limited education. Again, you cannot afford not to pursue your education.

REACHING YOUR EDUCATIONAL GOALS

Community colleges are a great place to start, or restart, your education. Especially in today's world and its need for trained specialists, more and more community colleges are offering extended certification programs in fields ranging from automobile technology to horticulture, computer coding, video game design, and nursing, just to name a few. It is well worth your time, energy, and priority to investigate your local community college, whether in person or online, to discover what it offers.

If getting a bachelor's degree is your goal, then beginning at a community college and transferring to a four-year college or university is a very attainable goal. Although people who start at a community college in the hopes of transferring to a four-year college tend to have lower college graduation rates than those who start at a four-year college, this should not deter you from starting your journey—remember, it's all about grit.

As I mentioned, I started at a community college and completed

CHAPTER 6: CHANGING TRAJECTORIES, FOR GENERATIONS

all my general education and prerequisite coursework before transferring to, and then graduating from, SDSU. Actually, a lot of people in the education profession do it this way. My college degree shows it is from SDSU, not two years at community college and two years at SDSU. No one knows, and frankly, no one cares that I started at a community college.

Education can change the trajectory of your and your family's life, for generations. There are a myriad of state and federal grant and loan opportunities and programs for people who cannot afford to pay cash upfront for their college education. If this is the case for you, I highly recommend speaking with your local community college financial aid department to see how much college will cost and how much you may be able to receive in both grant and loan money.

Seeing the difference in median income based on education levels, investing in your education just makes sense—and cents. And, in all honesty, as the following example will show, if you start at a community college and then transfer to a state college, the costs—not including living expenses and food—are actually very reasonable.

Community college per unit cost: $46
Approximate number of transferable units to a four-year college: 70
Total cost for community college tuition ($46 x 70): $3,220
Books per semester: $800
Total cost of books (five semesters at 14 units per semester): $4,000

Total costs (five semesters): $7,322

Four-year state college tuition (per year for unlimited units): $7,460
Books per semester: $800
Total cost of books (four semesters): $3,200

Total cost for tuition (four semesters, or two years): $14,920

Total costs (four semesters, or two years): $18,120

Other costs (parking, miscellaneous fees, etc.): $2,000

Total cost of college education (not including living expenses and food): $27,442

(Note: These numbers are just estimates; you will have to research your specific area to find more accurate numbers and figures).

Now, let's revisit the difference between someone who did not earn a high school diploma and a person with a bachelor's degree to see the return on your investment by pursuing your education. $4,624 per month (bachelor's degree) – $2,050 a month (less than a high school diploma) = $2,574 more per month.

1 year	$30,888 ($2,574 x 12 months)
5 years	$154,440
10 years	$308,880
20 years	$617,760
30 years	$926,664
40 years	$1,235,520
50 years	$1,544,440

In this scenario, within one year, you would have recouped the total cost of your college education. Within five years, your college education would have paid for itself six times over. And after fifty years, your college education would have paid for itself sixty times over. Talk about a long-haul perspective.

Yes, student loans are a major reason why many people are in debt. However, the problem many people face with student loans is that they attend private colleges or universities that are extremely expensive, thus they rack up an exorbitant amount of debt. Having a degree from SDSU, I have worked alongside—and even made more money than—people who went to expensive private colleges.

Another huge problem is when people borrow more money than they need and buy extraneous things. And sadly, some of these people start college or begin a certificated program, but never finish. By not finishing, they do not reap the financial benefits of having a college degree or certificate, but they are still required to pay back their loans—with interest.

Pursuing your education might well be a long-haul dream at this point, as we all know that a lot of life will happen between the time of reading these words and enrolling in your first class, let alone walking across the stage to receive your college diploma or certification. However, I am here to tell you: it can be done, and it is not as hard as you might think.

Therefore, if you love yourself, and if you love your family, remember Bob Goff's words of wisdom from the beginning of this chapter, "...it becomes clear that we need to stop plotting the course and instead just land the plane on our plans to make a difference by getting to the 'do' part of faith. That's because love is never stationary. In the end, love doesn't just keep thinking about it or keep planning for it. Simply put: love does."

Similar to grit, when moving toward "doing," instead of just "planning," what often makes the biggest difference is not our intelligence, but our mindset.

CHAPTER 7: MINDSETS

THE "UNCONSCIOUS HOLDOVER"

Remember, right thinking is the raw material for right actions. People's actions will naturally reveal the direction of their thoughts. Therefore, how has your thinking or mindset affected your current reality? What beliefs do you hold about yourself and your future that do not align with you being the best, healthiest version of yourself? What lies do you believe about yourself that are holding you back and making you doubt that you can be debt free and financially strong? How is your old way of thinking—your old paradigm—affecting your new way of thinking—your new paradigm?

In this vein of trying to create an environment where right thinking is the basis for right actions is the concept of the "unconscious holdover," and the effect it can have on new and relevant information when pitted against an older existing paradigm. Richard Tarnas (2001) explains, "Revolutions in human thought seldom take place in a single clean sweep…a paradigm shift, or break from the past—a kind of declaration of independence—will retain unexamined [unconscious] assumptions that limit the success of the new vision…like a mortgage imposed on the new paradigm by the historical circumstances of its origin" (p. 64).

Therefore, it's entirely possible that an old paradigm can threaten to destroy new thoughts, no matter how relevant, valuable, or true they really are. The "unconscious holdover" is a powerful concept and must be dealt with accordingly.

On a historical, global level, the "unconscious holdover" concept is sometimes related to an occurrence in WWI—a war that claimed the lives of over nine million people. In trying to understand the magnitude of the devastation during WWI, some historians identify the concept of the "ghost of Napoleon" as a major factor in the high number of war casualties. They state that the "ghost of Napoleon"— the old paradigm of battle—raged while being pitted against the new reality of modern weapons.

Those WWI weapons, like the machine gun, mustard gas, and tanks, created a new paradigm of warfare. However, both the Allies and the Central Powers continued to employ old war tactics that were based on Napoleonic strategies. For example, the old tactic of facing one's enemy, and having each side fire at the other was still being employed as a strategy. However, during WWI, instead of one soldier firing one shot and then reloading his rifle, a soldier operating a machine gun could now fire 400–600 rounds per minute.

During WWI, soldiers on both sides would "go over the top" of their trenches and, frantically and desperately, run through "no man's land" areas while being viciously mowed down by machine-gun fire. "No man's land" was the wasteland between the opposing armies' trenches, and this space was riddled with barbed wire and obese vermin masticating on the corpses of fallen soldiers. Reading the history books, we find that the "ghost of Napoleon" was very much alive at the Battle of the Somme.

The Battle of the Somme took place near France's Somme River between July 1 and November 1, 1916. During the very first hour of the battle, over 12,000 British soldiers were killed, and after that first day, over 57,000 British soldiers had lost their lives. This carnage then continued. During the four months of the battle, there were over one and a half million casualties on both sides. The "unconscious holdover" from the old paradigm didn't allow military leaders on either side to fully accept the new reality of modern weaponry, and the result was millions of deaths.

On a corporate level, the "unconscious holdover" concept can be related to the collapse of Blockbuster Video and the rise of Netflix. As we all know, the Internet created a new paradigm, and Blockbuster Video's business model—an old paradigm—was not congruent with the new reality of the Internet.

Remember the days of Blockbuster Video, where you had to leave your home in order to rent a movie? Then, if you wanted a new release, you would have to get to the store before it opened on the first day of the release, wait for the store to open, and then casually walk, but really, actually run, through the store to grab one of the newly released movies. If you did not get the new release on the first day it was released, sometimes it would take weeks to finally rent it.

Finally came the worst aspect of Blockbuster Video: returning the movies. In order to avoid late fees, you had to return new releases after two days, and all other movies after five days. I remember having to leave for work 15 minutes early simply to drop off the movies. Or, worse yet, was getting home after a long day at work and realizing that you had forgotten to return the movies. You then had to make that tough decision of paying the late fees or climbing back into your car and driving to the store to return the movies.

With the new reality of the Internet and the rise of Netflix, as well as numerous other streaming services today, people no longer have to leave their homes to watch a movie. Movies are always available or "in stock." There are no per-unit costs or late fees. And, finally, you never again have to get in your car and drive across town to return a movie.

Taking these two examples and applying them to our discussion, it is important to see how the "unconscious holdover" concept may be affecting the way you are living your life. Ask yourself whether your old way of thinking—your old paradigm—about money, yourself, and your future is affecting your new way of thinking and today's current reality—your new paradigm.

SHIFT HAPPENS: PARADIGMS

As soon as I was hired as a teacher, my goal was to both buy a house and get my master's degree within three years. My wife also had a goal of becoming a hairstylist. Therefore, with two children in elementary school, working as a full-time high school social science teacher, and with my wife attending cosmetology school five nights a week, I re-enrolled in college to pursue my master's degree. I went to night school two nights a week for 18 months straight to earn an M.S. in school counseling. Even though I felt like I was the personification of grit, those months were a very difficult and trying time in my life.

Nevertheless, through hard work, grit, and discipline, my wife and I were able to buy a house after my third year of teaching. Yet, even though things were improving financially for us, the "unconscious holdover" of my old paradigm of being poor, struggling, and constantly having nothing was hard to break free from. Actually, if I am being totally honest and transparent, it took nearly 20 years for me to finally be free of that old paradigm. For the longest time, I was only truly comfortable when I had a zero balance in my bank accounts—actually, really a zero balance in our family's checking account, as we never had any type of savings.

Having gone so many years paying all of our bills with only pennies left over at the end of each month, I had become quite comfortable having nothing. I was so used to being broke that I could not envision a future where I was not constantly struggling financially. I later found out that psychologists call this mindset "hedonic adaptation." Hedonic adaptation can occur with both positive and negative experiences, where, after repeated exposure to the same emotion-producing stimulus, people tend to experience less of the emotion. In other words, people get used to the bad, or to the good.

When experiencing a negative emotion-producing stimulus (i.e., constantly struggling financially), hedonic adaptation can be useful, as it can help build resilience and keep one motivated to achieve. This is what motivated me to go back to college, get my undergraduate degree, become a teacher, get my master's degree, and buy a house. However, by constantly struggling financially, I began to live how a lot of people live who constantly struggle financially: I lived for the moment.

About five years after we bought our house, the housing market in San Diego reached an all-time high. Because of this, the equity in our house grew substantially to over $250,000. As a result, banks started to contact us about equity lines of credit. Similar to a credit card, equity lines of credit allowed us to buy things we had never been able to purchase before.

At the same time, our credit card company increased our credit limit to $30,000. Although the increased equity in our home was awesome, the situation was bittersweet: through credit and a lack of discipline, we had begun to live well beyond our means. However, due to the "unconscious holdover" of my old paradigm, I subconsciously welcomed back the days of being in over my head and constantly struggling financially.

Like myself, I think that many people have a difficult time envisioning themselves and their finances differently than they currently are, especially if they have always struggled financially. I think people's "unconscious holdover" imposes a mortgage on the possibilities of a new reality, thus threatening to destroy people's new thoughts, no matter how relevant, valuable, or true they might be. Therefore, simply changing how you spend your money will not be enough. Remember, as I said at the outset, there are no quick fixes. You will also have to change how you view money, yourself, and your future. You will have to change your mindset.

GROWTH MINDSET

In her 2006 book, *Mindset: The New Psychology of Success*, Dr. Carol Dweck reveals years of research in discovering two very distinct mindsets: the fixed mindset, and the growth mindset. Supporting her theory about these two mindsets, Dweck provides examples of research documenting each one in action.

In one case, Dweck visited the University of Hong Kong, where everything is in English—the classes, the textbooks, and the exams. Since some students were not fully proficient in English, Dweck surmised that it would make sense for them to do something about it. Therefore, as the students arrived to register for their freshman year, Dweck, knowing which students were not fully proficient in English, asked the following question: "If the faculty offered a course for students who need to improve their English skills, would you take it?"

Dweck also measured these students' mindsets by asking them how much they agreed with statements like, "You have a certain amount of intelligence, and you can't really do much to change it." She found that people who agreed with this type of statement had a fixed mindset. However, Dweck found that those students who had a growth mindset agreed with other proposed statements, such as, "You can always substantially change how intelligent you are."

After asking the incoming freshmen these questions, Dweck shared her findings. She writes, "Later, we looked at who said 'yes' to the English classes. Students with the growth mindset said an emphatic 'yes.' But those with the fixed mindset were not very interested. Believing that success was about learning, students with the growth mindset seized the chance. But those with the fixed mindset didn't want to expose their deficiencies. Instead, to feel smart in the short run, they were willing to put their college careers at risk. This is how the fixed mindset makes people into non-learners" (pp. 17–18). This is exactly why Dweck says people with a fixed mindset may plateau early and achieve less than their full potential; it is because they are afraid to expose their deficiencies by seeking out help.

Throughout her book, Dweck provides both research and real-life examples of the fixed and growth mindsets at work in a variety of fields, including academia and the arts; sports; business; relationships; and parenting, teaching, and coaching.

For instance, Dweck discusses the fixed mindset when examining Billy Beane, the baseball player and, eventually, the manager of the 2002 Oakland Athletics, on which the movie *Moneyball* was based. Dweck explains that Beane, as a baseball player, was a natural, but he also lacked one thing: the mindset of a champion. Beane could not, and would not, accept failure, and as he moved up to more competitive leagues, every at-bat became a nightmare—another opportunity for humiliation. Innately, Beane's entire identity was teetering on his ability to perform.

With Beane's struggles as the backdrop, Dweck explains the thinking of a person with a fixed mindset: "Natural talent should not need effort. Effort is for the others, the less endowed. Natural talent does not ask for help. It is an admission of weakness. In short, the natural does not analyze his deficiencies and coach or practice them away. The very idea of deficiencies is terrifying" (p. 83).

In stark comparison, Dweck then discusses Michael Jordan. Dweck explains that Jordan was not a natural, but was arguably the hardest-working athlete in the sport of basketball. Jordan was actually cut from his high school varsity basketball team, wasn't recruited by the college he wanted to play for, and wasn't drafted by the first two NBA teams that could have chosen him. However, these setbacks never stopped him from pushing himself to become better. Through discipline, dedication, and, yes, practice, practice, and more practice,

Jordan became one of the greatest basketball players of all time.

Dweck writes, "For Jordan, success stems from the mind. [Jordan states,] 'The mental toughness and the heart are a lot stronger than some of the physical advantages you might have. I've always said that and I've always believed that.' But other people don't. They look at Michael Jordan and they see the physical perfection that led inevitably to his greatness" (p. 86). For Jordan, who personifies the growth mindset, effort is a prerequisite for success. Dweck continues, "Jordan knew how hard he had worked to develop his abilities. He was a person who had struggled and grown, not a person who was inherently better than others" (p. 32).

The fixed mindset sees intelligence as static: this person feels that intelligence is something very basic that cannot change. You can learn new things, but you can't really raise your intelligence. Because of this, the fixed mindset leads to a desire to "look smart," thereby creating a tendency to avoid challenges. Additionally, people are often defensive or give up easily when faced with obstacles, see effort as fruitless, ignore useful negative feedback, feel threatened by the success of others, and believe people cannot really change—in other words, that people can do things differently, but the important parts of who they are cannot be changed. As a result, people with a fixed mindset often plateau early and achieve less than their full potential (Dweck, 2006, pp. 12–13, 245).

On quite the other hand, the growth mindset sees intelligence as something that can be developed: no matter how much "intelligence" you have, you can always increase it significantly. You can always substantially change how intelligent you are. Because of this, the growth mindset leads to a desire to learn, thereby creating a tendency to embrace challenges, persist in the face of setbacks, see effort as the path to mastery, learn from useful negative feedback, find lessons and inspiration in the success of others, and believe that people can change—no matter who, people can always substantially change things about themselves. As a result, people with a growth mindset continue to reach ever-higher levels of achievement (Dweck, 2006, pp. 12–13, 245).

As Dweck has found, taking new action is at the heart of a person with a growth mindset because they embrace challenges, persist in the face of obstacles, see effort as a path to mastery, learn from criticism, and find lessons and inspiration in the successes of others. All of this motivates them to take new action. Conversely, taking new action seems to be the antithesis of a person with a fixed mindset because they avoid challenges, get defensive or give up easily, see effort as fruitless, ignore useful negative feedback, and feel threatened by the success of others. All of this motivates them to be protectors of the status quo, since this is where their comfort zone lies, and where, more than likely, they reign as king or queen.

Regardless of where you may fall on the spectrum of mindsets, speaking from a true growth mindset perspective, Dweck offers hope: "You have a choice. Mindsets are just beliefs. They're powerful beliefs, but they're just something in your mind, and you can always change your mind" (p. 16).

Finally, Dweck, through multiple experiments with hundreds of children, found that praising children's intelligence harms their motivation and performance. Dweck reports, "Yes, children love praise. And they especially love to be praised for their intelligence and talent. It really does give them a boost—but only for a moment. The minute they hit a snag, their confidence goes out the window and their motivation hits rock bottom. If success means they're smart, then failure means they're dumb" (p. 175).

Therefore, in order to assist people, whether children or adults, in developing a growth mindset, people should place a high priority on effort, perseverance, and grit (and not intelligence); these are things that people accomplish through practice, study, persistence, and having good strategies. Part of being successful in any endeavor—including in your financial life—is having a solid, firm, articulated plan.

A concrete plan.

PART II
HOW

CHAPTER 8: DEVELOPING CONCRETE PLANS

TRANSITION

Part I of this book set the stage and context for redesigning the reality of your finances. The premise of Part I was that there are no meaningful quick fixes in life that are likely to last—that good things take time, energy, and should be made a priority. This requires a long-haul perspective. For many people, simply applying financial principles without understanding *why* they do what they do will only yield short-term gains. Without the foundation of *why*, suggestions are like fad diets: the diet may work initially, but if eating healthier and exercising regularly are not ingrained into one's lifestyle, it will likely fail.

Chapter 1 discussed how the money and time spent on buying and reading this book would be well worth the investment, even if readers took just one thing from this book and applied it to their life in a positive way. It also discussed that it is not necessarily how much money people have that matters, but rather, it is how they spend their money that matters most. The chapter ended by encouraging readers to pursue deep and honest reflection about their situation, and then use this book as a road map to get themselves out of debt, become financially free, and make a plan for their futures.

Chapter 2 discussed the "myth of adolescence," and how people never expect bad things to happen to them, including being in excessive debt. It also discussed how people have freedom of choice, but not of consequence, and how today is not forever—that things can change for the better. Additionally, it showed how right thinking is the raw material for right actions, and that people's actions will naturally reveal the direction of their thoughts. The chapter ended by discussing the importance of planning for the future by having adequate insurance so that people could protect themselves, their loved ones, and their assets.

Chapter 3 talked about the debt matrix and how people's systems of spending are perfectly designed to get the results they get. It encouraged readers to unplug from the debt matrix and become a Neo in order to be the change they wish to see in their financial life. The chapter further encouraged people to take a hard, honest look at *why* they spend their money the way they do. It ended by asking people to reflect on any perceived voids in their life and how such voids might be connected to the *why* of their spending habits.

Chapter 4 delved deeper into some of the possible reasons as to the *why* of people's behavior by discussing the adverse childhood experiences (ACEs) study. It further considered trauma and its potential effects on people over the course of their lifespan. The chapter ended by encouraging people to identify *why* they do what they do (including spending money) through deep and honest reflection, which can allow them to be the best, healthiest version of themselves in all aspects of life.

Chapter 5 discussed how a person's biggest asset is themselves. Therefore, the chapter encouraged readers to invest in themselves, including their education. The chapter further illustrated the difference of income based on education levels and the negative effects of poverty as a means of encouraging people to pursue their education so that they are able to change the trajectory of their lives, as well as their family's, potentially, for generations to come.

Chapter 6 discussed grit and the power of perseverance in going after and obtaining long-haul goals. It further reviewed the importance of pursuing one's education and showed how inexpensive attending college could be, particularly when one begins in community college, especially when compared to the far greater earning potential that more education can generate.

Chapter 7 looked at mindsets and introduced the concept of the "unconscious holdover"—how old paradigms (i.e., old ways of thinking) can threaten to destroy new thoughts, no matter how relevant, valuable, or true they really are. It also discussed hedonic adaptation, and how people, over time, get used to life being a certain way, whether good or bad. The chapter ended by discussing the power of having a growth mindset.

Part II of this book presents more concrete concepts and suggestions related to people's finances. Through the use of these concrete plans, people can choose to take, tweak, adapt, alter, apply, and anchor the ideas and suggestions to fit their particular needs and situations. Part II considers the *how* of redesigning the reality of your finances.

CONCRETE PLANS FOR "NOT YET" PRACTICES

Using the growth mindset discussed in Chapter 7 as a foundation, I would like to challenge you to take just one concept from this book and practice it, giving yourself permission to fail. I will refer to this as a "Not Yet" Practice. Then, if you do fail, you can begin to realize that growth only occurs through effort. It will then be time to try again. And again. And again. Once you master the first "Not Yet" Practice—and it becomes part of your repertoire, routine, and mindset—then tackle another one.

Remember, the growth mindset is about practice and learning, so when setbacks do occur, it is vital to reflect and ask yourself these questions: "What can I learn from this?" and "What will I do next time when I am in this situation?" As Dweck (2006) writes, "It's a learning process—not a battle between the bad you and the good you" (p. 241). This is in stark contrast to dealing with setbacks with a fixed mindset response, which leads people to beat themselves up and feel that they are incompetent, weak, or bad.

Here, the word "practice" is used very deliberately because "not yet" denotes something that has not yet been achieved, but will be reached, eventually, through effort. The following are some definitions of "practice" found on the Internet. As you read these definitions, notice how intertwined and integral "practice" is to the growth mindset and the concept of "not yet":

- The actual application or use of an idea, belief, or method as opposed to theories about such application or use.

- The repeated exercise in or performance of an activity or skill so as to acquire or maintain proficiency in it.

- To perform an activity or exercise a skill repeatedly or regularly in order to improve or maintain one's proficiency.

- To carry out or perform a particular activity, method, or custom habitually or regularly.

Finally, Kerry Howells (2012) offers some words of wisdom related to the idea of practice: "As the saying goes, 'practice makes perfect,' but this does not mean that our practice *is* perfect. If it was, we would not need to practice any more" (p. 49).

However, simply saying you're going to practice or do something is not enough. This is why Dweck (2006) recommends making vivid, concrete plans. The following is Dweck's recommendation and rationale for making vivid, concrete plans over simply vowing to do something: "Think of something you need to do, something you want to learn, or a problem you have to confront. What is it? Now make a concrete plan. *When* will you follow through on your plans? *Where* will you do it? *How* will you do it? Think about it in vivid detail. These concrete plans—plans you can visualize—about *when, where,* and *how* you are going to do something lead to really high levels of follow-through, which, of course, ups the chances of success" (p. 228).

Furthermore, as Dweck points out, it is important to read over the differences between the fixed and growth mindsets every day (see Chapter 7). By doing so, you can reinforce the development of the growth mindset while simultaneously prevent some of the fixed mindset thoughts to creep in when you are confronted with a setback.

Utilizing Dweck's recommendations, we can use the "formula" below to articulate your vivid, concrete plan for your first "Not Yet" Practice. Then we can move on to the next. And another one after that. In order for the practice to be fulfilled, you may have to write down your plan, tape it to your mirror, ask someone to remind and encourage you daily to follow through, or set it as a reminder on your phone. Basically, do whatever is necessary to keep the "Not Yet" Practice in the forefront of your mind.

- WHAT do I need or want to improve?

- WHEN will I do it?

- WHERE will I do it?

- HOW will I do it?

Once again, after 47 years, I am finally beginning to understand that all good things in life are found in the long haul: relationships, health, spirituality, wisdom, finances, and so much more. Things—good things—simply take time, energy, and priority to become better, or even great.

Having a plan, which requires action, is an important part of this process. Believing that good things can become better through effort is at the core of the growth mindset. Therefore, firmly believing in the less-is-more paradox, your first "Not Yet" Practice should be based on something relatively small so that you can begin to build a foundation for success. If our goals are too lofty initially, we may succumb to the all-too-familiar arsenal that fortifies the status quo: "Well, that didn't work." If, from the very beginning, we are not careful as we create a vivid, concrete plan that is attainable, the continual cycle of trying and failing will only have a bigger and deeper negative impact on our perceived ability for growth. For the fixed mindset person, this type of thinking can easily transition from an action—"I failed"—to an identity—"I am a failure" (Dweck, 2006, p. 33).

In terms of changing one's mindset and connecting it to these "Not Yet" Practices, Dweck offers some sage advice that we should all keep in mind as we traverse a life that is full of highs and lows, triumphs and defeats: "When people drop the good-bad, strong-weak thinking that grows out of the fixed mindset, they're better able to learn useful strategies that help with self-control [or discipline]. Every lapse doesn't spell doom. It's like anything else in the growth mindset. It's a reminder that you're an unfinished human being and a clue to how to do it better next time" (p. 242).

EXAMPLE OF A CONCRETE PLAN FOR A "NOT YET" PRACTICE

After reading Chapter 3 and diligently charting all your expenses for a one- or two-month period, let's say you realize you were spending a lot of money eating out during your lunch break at work. By charting your expenses, you identified that you ate lunch out an average of three days per week, spending approximately $8 each time.

Keeping the less-is-more paradox in mind, you decide to start small by reducing just the number of days you eat lunch out each week by one day. By doing so, you will save $32 a month ($8 a week x 4 weeks). Surprisingly, after looking at your budget, you realize the $32 saved is basically the cost of your monthly online subscriptions to Netflix, Hulu, and X-Box Live combined. Awesome!

By starting small and seeing how your effort, good strategy, and change in behavior will pay off in other areas of your life, you will increase your level of success in the long haul. If you leave no room for error in the beginning and eliminate all instances of going out to eat during your lunch break, then when—not if—you fail, it will be all too easy to give up and say, "Well, that didn't work."

Pouncing on the one instance of failure could also be the result of the ugly lie from the "unconscious holdover" of your old paradigm that whispers, "You are a failure." Therefore, start small, build on your successes, rebuke the lie, speak positively about yourself to yourself, and try to find someone who will help you meet your goal. That person should be someone you can trust, confide in, and candidly share with when you struggle and fail, and one who has your best interests in mind. Now, make your concrete plan.

WHAT DO I NEED OR WANT TO IMPROVE?

While at work, I only want to eat lunch out twice a week. Three times a week I will bring my lunch from home.

WHEN WILL I DO IT?

Since I have the weekend to go shopping and prepare food for the week, the following will be my lunch plan for the week:

Monday—bring lunch
Tuesday—bring lunch
Wednesday—bring lunch
Thursday—eat out

Friday—eat out

WHERE WILL I DO IT?

When I do go out to lunch, I will try to eat at places that cost under $8 in order to try to save even more money.

HOW WILL I DO IT?

I will go shopping for lunch items during the weekend so that I am prepared for the week. When I go out to eat, I will only use cash or my debit card. If, for some reason, I have to go out to eat on a day I had planned to bring my lunch, I will switch days so that I do not go over my two days per week of going out to eat.

Trust me, after one to three months of living out this concrete plan, your confidence will go up, you will have more money in your pocket, and you may even lose a little weight from cutting back on all the eating out. At that point, if you are feeling confident and want to save even more money, reduce the number of days you go out to eat by one more day. In doing so, you may realize that the additional $32 saved a month can fill up your gas tank. Then, you will have built momentum and can begin to look for other ways to cut expenses and save money. However, developing concrete plans is one thing; sticking to them is another. This is why the key to redesigning the reality of your finances will be discipline.

CHAPTER 9: DISCIPLINE

A HARD TRUTH

Building upon Part I of this book, we need to turn our attention to the importance of discipline. Discipline is training yourself to do things in a controlled and habitual way. Regarding your finances, discipline may require you to give up certain things, go without particular "comforts," work harder or put in more hours, do things differently, create and stick to concrete plans, delay gratification, and sacrifice now in order to benefit later, to name a few.

Without discipline, no advice, suggestions, books, apps, counseling, or even more money will keep you out of excessive debt. As a case in point, according to the National Endowment for Financial Education, an astounding 70 percent of people who win a lottery or get a big lump sum cash payout actually ends up broke within a few years.

A hard truth is that when it comes to almost anything in life—including finances—other people cannot want something more for you than you want it for yourself. People cannot want you to be better off financially more than you want it for yourself. Ultimately, people make their own decisions and live their own lives. Again, people have freedom of choice, not of consequence.

Therefore, if you are serious about redesigning the reality of your finances, you will need to develop a disciplined, long-haul commitment to that goal. Not only that, but if you are married or have a significant other, then discussing, developing, and agreeing together on a course of action will be paramount in lowering the frequency of possible hurt feelings, frustrations, and arguments while concurrently upping the chances of success.

ESTABLISH A BUDGET

Creating and sticking to a budget will be paramount for successfully redesigning the reality of your finances. Whether professionally or personally, whenever I establish a budget, I always estimate low for income and high for expenses to safeguard myself from going over that budget. Then, when it turns out my actual income is higher, and true expenses are lower than originally budgeted, I have a nice little extra chunk of change instead of a deficit.

Since there is no "Golden Rule" on how much to budget for various expenses, the following are some general guidelines when preparing your budget. Again, knowing one book could never fully satisfy the needs of all people, please note all these scenarios are relative. For example, if the percentages seem too high or too low in certain categories, then simply readjust so that they fit your particular situation.

That said, in order to live within your means without using credit to supplement your income, increasing the amount to spend in one area must mean decreasing that same amount in one or more areas. Also important to note is that if you have a large amount of debt, then you may choose to lower certain percentages or temporarily eliminate certain categories—although not any of your insurance policies—in order to first pay off those high and compounding interest debts. Therefore, as you read the following, try to relate the information and percentages to your own situation as best you can.

First, based on your tax bracket, budget the percentage to be taken out for taxes based on your gross monthly income, or pretax income. For this example, I will use 15 percent for taxes.

Second, budget 25 to 30 percent for your mortgage or rent (i.e., housing) based on your gross monthly income. If paying a mortgage, this amount should include your property taxes; private mortgage insurance (PMI), if needed; homeowners insurance; principal payments; and interest. Homeowners' association (HOA) fees should also be included in this amount for both homeowners and renters who must make these recurring payments. Anything more than 30 percent may cause you to run the risk of spending too much on housing, which can leave you too little for other expenses and your ability to reach your financial goals.

Third, budget 10 to 15 percent based on your gross monthly income for investing in your future (i.e., retirement).

Fourth, budget 10 to 15 percent based on your gross monthly income for debt, such as car loans, student loans, or credit card debt.

Fifth, budget 20 to 25 percent based on your gross monthly income for personal needs and wants: health insurance, car insurance, an emergency fund, six months' worth of bills, groceries, gas or other transportation costs, utilities, vacations, charitable contributions, and any others.

Finally, the remaining money from your gross monthly income can go toward entertainment: eating out, online subscriptions (Netflix, Hulu, X-Box Live, etc.), clothing, toys and gadgets, and other similar things.

Therefore, if you took the averages of each of the previous budgeted categories (27.5 percent for housing + 12.5 percent for retirement + 12.5 percent for debt + 22.5 percent for savings and other personal needs), you would have budgeted 75 percent of your gross monthly income. Seventy-five percent plus 15 percent for taxes equals 90 percent, thus leaving you 10 percent of your gross monthly income for entertainment.

As one can see, the less debt you have, the more money you have for investing in your future, for savings and personal needs, and for entertainment. Based on this suggested budget, if you had no debt besides your mortgage or rent, that would mean you would have an additional 10 to 15 percent of your gross monthly income that could be repurposed for whatever you wanted.

Now, if you are a homeowner, imagine the day when you make your final mortgage payment, thus allowing you to be 100 percent debt free. You will have an additional 35 to 45 percent of your gross monthly income to do whatever you please. Please note, this reality does not only exist for people who have retired; this reality can exist for you much sooner than you might think.

INCOME AND EXPENSES

The first step in redesigning the reality of your finances is to get a clear picture of how much you make, how much you spend, and exactly how you spend your money. I always like to use a zero-balance budget. A zero-balance budget is where every single dollar of your income is accounted for. When creating a zero-balance budget, be sure to account for expenses that may not occur every month like income, home, and other taxes; health, home, and car insurance; memberships dues; and others that will need to be averaged into your monthly zero-balance budget. Therefore, whether on your computer or in a journal, account for all your income and expenses for a one-month period of time.

Depending on the person, creating a budget can be a lengthy and complex process. Therefore, in order to provide some context, the following is an average, simplified, monthly budget example of someone who has been living beyond their means. This example demonstrates how people get into excessive debt and remain plugged into the debt matrix. However, this example also illustrates how people—through discipline—can unplug from the debt matrix and redesign the reality of their finances.

The following example is based on a fictitious character we can call Jason. Jason is 29 years old. He graduated from high school and attended community college for about two years, although he never got his degree. Jason lives by himself in the downtown area. Although he has a decent-paying job, his work does not provide any sort of retirement benefits. However, it does provide health insurance, for which Jason must pay a monthly premium.

Gross (pretax) income: $3,177

Net income:
Income after 15 percent taxes ($477) taken out: $2,700

Fixed expenses:
Rent/mortgage (including water and trash): $1,200
Utilities (gas and electric): $120
Cell phone: $80
Internet: $80
Health insurance: $120
Car insurance: $110
Cable TV: $200
Online subscriptions (i.e., Netflix, Hulu, and X-Box Live): $25

Total fixed expenses: $1,935

Variable expenses:
Groceries: $300
Gas: $120
Entertainment: $300
Miscellaneous: $45

Total variable expenses: $765

Total expenses (fixed + variable): $2,700

Balance (fixed + variable expenses - income = zero-balance budget): $0

In looking at Jason's example, do you notice anything missing besides savings and investing in his future? It's missing debt payments. This is where people get buried in excessive debt: they have more expenses than income, so they supplement their income through credit. Unfortunately, without discipline and without having an emergency fund or substantial savings, people can quickly get into trouble. The following is one example of how excessive debt accumulates for many people, including our Jason.

Jason goes out on a Friday night and spends $60 on drinks, dinner, and a movie. By doing so, he just spent 20 percent of his monthly allotted entertainment money in one night. (This is just one example; it does not have to be a night out on the town. This money could also be spent on purchasing clothing, video games, or a new tool or gadget.)

Therefore, if Jason were going to try to stay within his budget, he would have to limit himself to spending $8 a day for the next 29 days. This is something very few people can do. So, what usually happens? When Jason runs out of cash but wants to go out, he will use his credit card. This same scenario could be applied to when people run out of cash but need to buy groceries, have their car fixed, need house repairs, buy shoes for their kids, and so on. Consequently, credit card and other such debt payments now become part of Jason's monthly expenses. Jason's income becomes even more spread out, forcing him into a cyclical pattern of using credit to pay for more and more of his variable expenses, since the new, fixed expense of a credit card payment will now be added to his budget.

Making matters worse is that his credit is poor, due to having too many credit cards and being able to sometimes make only the minimum payments. As a result, Jason is a credit risk, and most businesses will only give him credit or loan him money at higher interest rates. This causes Jason to waste even more money on interest. Finally, unable to make his payments, Jason begins to rack up late fees and sometimes even overdraft bank fees, since different bills are being pulled from his account at different times through his auto-pay banking option. Our man Jason is now riddled with debt.

Jason has a choice to make: he can take the blue pill and continue to live in the debt matrix and be insane—doing the same things over and over while expecting different results—or Jason can take the red pill and, with discipline and grit, unplug from the debt matrix and change his systems of spending through wisdom—learning from his past in order to make better decisions for his future. In this way, Jason can redesign the reality of his finances.

CUT FIXED EXPENSES

Fixed expenses are expenditures that recur every month for about the same amount (e.g., rent or mortgage payments, cell phone plans, insurance, cable, and online subscriptions, to name a few). Whether on your computer or in a journal, write down all your fixed expenses; the monthly amounts; and if 1) they are absolutely essential for living; 2) they are highly desirable, or even required; or 3) they are something you do not have to have, but enjoy having.

Fixed Expense	Monthly amount	Priority (1, 2, Or 3)

About seven years ago, I had an epiphany: I can give myself a raise whenever I wanted by simply eliminating certain fixed expenses. Although I will not make more money, I can redirect the money saved to other places, thus allowing me to have more money at my disposal. For example, like Jason's situation, when I did this exercise and listed all my fixed expenses, the $200 per month I was spending on cable TV was low hanging fruit and became an easy target for elimination. So, I called the cable company (which also provided my Internet) and canceled my cable TV. I instantly had an extra $200 a month at my disposal. Not only that, but I also decided to play "hardball" by threatening to cancel my Internet service as well and look for a cheaper provider elsewhere. Knowing that I was serious because I had just canceled my cable TV, the sales representative immediately routed me to the "manager."

In the end, the "manager" and I were able to negotiate a deal where they offered to lower my Internet charges $20 a month in hopes to keep me as a customer. Now, I had $220 a month at my disposal. As I will discuss later, this is where discipline is paramount for your financial success. Having this "extra" $220 did not mean I could now go out and buy a newer car with a payment of $220 a month. Buying a newer car may have fulfilled a certain need, or even a void in my life, but, in the long haul, it would not have improved my financial reality.

Therefore, look at your fixed expenses listed under Priority 3 (and maybe even some under Priority 2) to determine which ones you can reduce, or even eliminate. If you are having a hard time deciding on something to lower or do away with, think about this: Would you rather live without those one or two things, or would you rather live with the chronic stress and anxiety that often accompanies excessive debt? Remember, be disciplined and be in this for the long haul.

A final note here, if you do use credit cards and have several, it may well be worth your time and energy to call those card companies and simply ask to have your interest rate lowered. If they say no, if you are able, calmly tell them that you will pay off the balance and then request to have them deactivate your card. Most credit card companies do not want to lose your business, so they will more than likely work with you. Better yet, always pay off your balance every month, thus making your interest rate a moot point. The best option, of course, is never to use a credit card unless you are in an extreme emergency.

CUT VARIABLE EXPENSES

Variable expenses are expenditures controlled by you that may or may not occur every month (e.g., groceries, gas, entertainment, vacations, going out to eat, clothing, and so forth). Again, whether on your computer or in a journal, write down all your variable expenses; the monthly amounts; and whether they are something that could be lowered or eliminated (at least, eliminated temporarily, as you work on decreasing your debt), and if so, then by how much.

Variable Expense	Monthly amount	Lower or eliminate; if so, by how much

If you completed the activity in Chapter 3 that charted your expenses for a one- or two-month period, then you should have a good idea where your money is going and how much you are currently spending on variable expenses. If you thought being disciplined was important with fixed expenses, discipline with variable expenses is absolutely paramount in redesigning the reality of your finances. This is true because most fixed expenses are mandatory for living a safe and protected life, whereas most variable expenses have to do with the choices people make on a day-to-day basis.

Once you have charted your variable expenses and have seen how much you spend in certain areas, it is now time to decide how much you can cut back. By cutting back, you will be able to take the money saved and apply it to your debt. Addressing the *why* of your spending was step one. Step two will be creating a concrete plan and having the discipline to stick to it.

Coupled with the epiphany that I could give myself a raise whenever I wanted by simply eliminating certain fixed expenses, when I did this exercise, I realized that my wife and I were spending a lot of money on one of the largest variable expenses—going out to eat. To combat this, we decided to utilize a strategy from Dave Ramsey (2011) called the "envelope technique" for our variable expenses.

THE ENVELOPE TECHNIQUE

After eliminating all unnecessary fixed expenses, it will be important to utilize a zero-balance budget and account for your remaining fixed expenses. You must then decide how much you want and what amount you are able to put toward debt, and then account for that amount in your zero-balance budget. In doing so, it may be wise to leave at least a little room for error.

Remember the less-is-more paradox: do not begin with expectations that are too high and, perhaps, too unrealistic. Rather, start small and build a foundation of success. Next, account for all the other categories in your budget: housing, investing in your future, and personal needs and wants. Finally, with whatever money is remaining for the month or week (depending on how and when you get paid), distribute it into envelopes for your variable expenses.

You should have envelopes for: 1) groceries; 2) gas or transportation costs (e.g., bus, subway, or trolley fares); 3) home supplies and toiletries; and 4) entertainment, including going out to eat and other miscellaneous items or situations. Feel free to add other envelopes as necessary; the point is to only use cash (or your debit card) for all these items with the goal being to use the rest of your income on paying down debt.

Regardless of how many envelopes you utilize, when the money from an envelope is gone, then it is gone. No more spending money unless you are willing to take some money from one of your other envelopes. The point is to use cash or your debit card—not credit—for all your variable expenses.

A cashless society is becoming more and more of a reality in today's world. Therefore, if taking cash out of your bank to implement the envelope technique does not align with your current ways of spending (e.g., if you mostly use a debit card for your purchases), then I highly recommend tracking the spending of your variable expenses daily using either an app or a spreadsheet. Especially in the beginning, when you are becoming more disciplined, it will be important to keep track of how much you are spending in each variable expense category you have established on a daily basis; again, this list includes groceries, transportation costs, home supplies, entertainment, and any others. If you do not, then all your money will be lumped into one sum, making it more difficult to get a clear picture of how much you are spending on the different variable expense categories you have established.

Thus, if you use a debit card instead of cash for the envelope technique, then I recommend having one specific bank account connected to your debit card for your variable expenses; a separate bank account for fixed expenses; and yet another separate bank account for emergencies, saving for your future, and money designated to pay off debt. If you do not do this, then all your funds will be merged together, likely resulting in you spending more money than you have allocated for your variable expenses. This is why I prefer and highly recommend using cash and the envelope technique.

As a teacher, I got paid only once per month, but I found it easier to use cash for the envelope technique on a weekly basis. Therefore, once it was decided how much my wife and I would use weekly for our various variable expenses, we would only put that amount of cash in each respective envelope every Sunday night—we used Sundays as our last day of the week. In the very beginning, when we were not as disciplined, we would leave the money for the other weeks in the bank and would only withdraw the next week's money on Sunday night. This ensured that we would not accidentally spend it prematurely.

By addressing the *why* of our spending systems, utilizing the envelope technique, being dedicated to eliminating our debt, and being disciplined, my wife and I were able to allocate (or squeeze out) an additional $325 per month from our variable spending. Combined with the $220 saved by eliminating cable TV and the reduction in the amount we were paying for our Internet, we now had an additional $545 per month that we could put toward building an emergency fund, paying off debt, and saving for our futures.

EMERGENCY FUNDS

After eliminating unnecessary fixed expenses, managing day-to-day variable expenses through the envelope technique to save money that could be applied to debt, and establishing and following a zero-balance budget, the next major step is to create an emergency fund. Emergency funds are essential. Emergency funds are to be used for situations that require you to spend more money than you have accounted for in your monthly budget, for example, in car expenses.

In many places, particularly outside of city centers, cars are essential because they are the means of taking people to their workplaces to earn a living. When a car needs to be repaired, it is not something people can really save up for. Usually, if it is not running, it needs to be fixed immediately. Therefore, instead of putting the expense on a high-interest-rate credit card, people can tap their emergency fund to pay for the repairs. The same can be said about people's health and homes. Emergencies should not be, "Man, I really need some baby back ribs right now, so let's go out."

Ramsey (2011) suggests that $1,000 would be a good starting place for an emergency fund, and I agree. However, if you do not own a car or a home, then maybe $1,000 is too high of an initial goal. Conversely, if you own multiple cars and your home, then $1,000 may not be enough to cover the myriad expenses that could arise with owning such assets.

The bottom line is to have enough cash on hand to pay for things when they come up and to avoid using credit. Eventually, you will also want to have approximately six months' worth of fixed and variable expenses saved in case you lose your job, get injured and can't work, or must deal with some other unforeseen event that threatens your ability to pay your bills.

CREDIT CARDS

There are a lot of different thoughts about the use of credit cards. For me, once again, it all comes down to whether you are disciplined or not. If you are using credit cards to supplement your income and are not able to pay the entire balance in full at the end of each month, then stop using credit cards immediately.

As will be discussed in Chapter 10, the amount of money you pay in interest (i.e., compounding interest) simply takes money out of your pocket in the long haul. Instead, as previously discussed, you really need to establish and follow a zero-balance budget, cut fixed and variable expenses, utilize the envelope technique, create an emergency fund, and begin to live within your means without the use of credit cards.

With the understanding that one book could never fully satisfy the needs of all people, I list some positive and negative consequences of using credit cards below. As you read this list, using honest reflection, decide if you are disciplined enough to take advantage of the positive consequences. On the other hand, if you fall victim to the negative consequences far too often, then do not use credit cards until you become more disciplined.

Some credit card companies offer "benefits" like travel miles, cash back, and other special offers. If you are disciplined, these can add up to some nice savings and travel benefits. However, such "benefits" are only worth the difference between how much you paid in interest and how much the "benefit" is worth. For example, if you "earned" $100 cash back, but you paid $500 in interest, you really did not "earn" anything. Rather, you fell victim to the credit card company's marketing ploy and actually lost $400. For every person that "earns" $100, there are hundreds, if not thousands, who will owe $400 (or far, far more) in interest.

Nowadays, practically every bill can be paid online using a credit card. If you are disciplined, you can use your credit card to pay your bills, and then pay off your credit card balance in full every month. Not only will you "earn" extra "benefits" from your credit card company, but this can often alleviate the numerous late and overdraft fees that some people accrue by having their bills on auto-pay, which draws on their debit card or checking account throughout the month, where they may or may not have sufficient funds. Note: if you feel you are not disciplined and will not be able to pay off your credit card balance in full every month, I recommend that you do not pay your bills online using a credit card.

Finally, I suggest that everyone have at least one credit card for extreme emergencies. However, what constitutes an emergency may vary from person to person, so really consider using this credit card only for significant difficulties that come out of the blue. For example, not having the perfect outfit for your second date is not an emergency, nor is getting the latest iPhone, nor is that craving for baby back ribs.

For me, an emergency would be related to you and your family's health, your ability to get to and from work in your automobile, or repairing or preventing more and longer-term damage to your home if it requires immediate repairs (e.g., the roof is leaking, a water or sewer pipe bursts, the water heater goes out, etc.). A great way to avoid having to use a credit card is to become more disciplined and to either decrease your expenses or increase your income—or better yet, both.

INCREASE YOUR INCOME

As previously discussed, you can "increase" your income and give yourself a raise by simply lowering or eliminating fixed and variable expenses. However, if need be, you can also increase your income by working additional hours or by finding a second job. Although not the most desirable thing to do, working more will provide you with the extra income to begin chipping away at debt, which, eventually, will put more money in your pocket once that debt is eliminated.

The same can be said about selling some of your belongings. Whether online or through an app, newspaper, or garage sale, you can sell those items that you no longer need or can do without. The increased income from working additional hours or a second job and the extra money from selling superfluous things should be aimed primarily at building your emergency fund and reducing or eliminating all debt.

Even while teaching, I constantly looked for ways to earn extra money. I earned my master's degree, which moved me up the pay scale. I always applied to teach summer school. I worked on school-related projects outside of the school day to earn curriculum writing pay. I earned a stipend by supporting new teachers through the Beginning Teacher Support and Assessment (BTSA) program. I taught extra classes whenever they were available. And I worked as an adult school administrator at night. I did whatever I needed to do in order to take care of my family and be as financially free as possible. Basically, I was disciplined.

After recognizing the *why* of your spending, being disciplined will allow you to engage more fully in the next phase: eliminating debt. Eliminating debt will be the powder keg for building the momentum you will need in order to redesign the reality of your finances.

Becoming disciplined and planning for your future is key when redesigning the reality of your finances. Therefore, no matter how much money you make, if you need assistance in creating and sticking to concrete plans in order to get out—and stay out—of debt, then please visit redesignthereality.com for more information.

CHAPTER 10: ELIMINATING DEBT AND INVESTING

BUILDING MOMENTUM

After lowering or eliminating unnecessary fixed expenses, managing day-to-day variable expenses through the envelope technique in order to save money that can be applied to existing debt, establishing and following a zero-balance budget, and creating an emergency fund so you stop using credit for emergencies, the next important step is to begin to eliminate debt.

If you have successfully implemented the first four steps, then this step is actually very exciting, as you will begin to see and feel the momentum building in your favor by paying off debt. Again, knowing that one book could never fully satisfy the needs of all people, please understand that the scenarios I discuss here are relative. Therefore, as you read the following, try to relate the information to your individual situation as best you can.

When it comes to eliminating debt and investing, different people have different theories. As will be discussed, compound interest can be either a person's best friend or their worst enemy. When it comes to credit card debt, however, compound interest will always be the latter—your worst enemy. For this reason, some people say it is critical to eliminate debt that has the highest interest rate first. Others, such as Ramsey (2011), explain that it is best to eliminate the smallest debt first, regardless of the interest rate. And still others say to eliminate the debt that will put the most money back into your pocket (i.e., the debt that has the highest monthly payment). Once again, for me, it all depends on how disciplined and invested you are in redesigning the reality of your finances.

For example, if you are finally at a point where you consider yourself disciplined (i.e., you are living within your means, learning to delay gratification, lowering or eliminating certain "comforts," putting the money saved by lowering or eliminating expenses toward debt and not toward new debt, creating and sticking to concrete plans, and willing to sacrifice now in order to benefit later), then I would suggest paying off small debts first in order to gain a sense of accomplishment and victory. Then, I would pay off debt that will put the most money back into my pocket.

By tasting victory, by eliminating some of your smaller debt and the debt that will put the most money back into your pocket first, you will have built momentum. Once disciplined, this momentum becomes more and more powerful as you simply continue to live within your means while rolling all the money you have saved by paying off debt toward other debt. Once all smaller debt has been paid off, you can then apply your increased disposable income toward tackling those larger debt items, like cars, student loans, and mortgages. Or, even more importantly, by saving it so that you invest in your future.

ELIMINATING DEBT

With all the information in mind thus far, let's go back to the example of Jason in Chapter 9. After living under the stress and anxiety of excessive debt, Jason finally decided to take the red pill and unplug from the debt matrix. However, since Jason has freedom of choice and not of consequence, his prior decisions left him straddled with some unwanted debt:

VISA balance: $5,000
VISA minimum payment: $125
MASTERCARD balance: $2,000
MASTERCARD minimum payment: $50
TARGET balance: $500
TARGET minimum payment: $15
WALMART balance: $400
WALMART minimum payment: $15

(Note: To simplify, these figures are rough estimates and do not reflect accrued interest.)

After looking at his fixed expenses, Jason decided to get rid of cable TV. However, through honest reflection, Jason realized that by getting rid of cable television and trying not to go out as much, he would need more things to occupy his time. Therefore, he decided to keep all of his online subscriptions (i.e., Netflix, Hulu, and X-Box Live).

Furthermore, Jason decided all his other fixed expenses were required and could not be lowered or eliminated, with the possible exception of where he was living, since he was spending approximately 38 percent of his gross monthly income on housing. (Recall from Chapter 9 that housing should be 25 to 30 percent of your gross monthly income.) Regardless, Jason was able to squeeze out $200 in fixed expenses that could then be applied to his outstanding debt.

After looking at his variable expenses, Jason made concrete plans to eat in more and make things from scratch, thus saving even more by not buying prepackaged meals. Jason also made a commitment to himself to save even more money by going out less, thereby allowing him to save money on gas. Therefore, Jason was able to reduce groceries by $50, reduce entertainment by $125, reduce gas by $25, and roll the $45 for miscellaneous expenses into paying down his debt by

CHAPTER 10: ELIMINATING DEBT AND INVESTING   99

either simply doing without or by finding creative, free alternatives for certain items.

Therefore, Jason was able to squeeze out $245 in variable expenses that could then be applied to his debt. By reprioritizing, Jason now had $445 a month to put toward paying off his balances ($200 from fixed expenses + $245 from variable expenses = $445). As an unintended benefit, Jason also noticed he had more energy, and even lost some weight from not eating out as much and by not eating as many prepackaged meals.

Unfortunately, by having more expenses than income, Jason had missed several months of payments on all his credit cards. Therefore, the first thing he did was to begin making the minimum payments while also putting the balance from the $445 into an emergency fund. He decided that he should have at least $500 in his emergency fund. Therefore, after paying the $205 in minimum payments toward his debt, he took the remaining $240 and put it into his emergency fund. After two months (and fortunately, avoiding any unforeseen issues), Jason had $480 of the $500 in his emergency fund while he had also been chipping away at his credit card balances.

During the third month, with his emergency fund close to being fully funded at $480, Jason had the full $445 to put toward debt. Going after the smallest debt first in order to build momentum, Jason decided to pay off his WALMART credit card. After making the combined minimum payments to the other three credit cards (VISA, MASTERCARD, and TARGET) of $190, Jason went into WALMART and applied the remaining $255 to his balance. Jason now only owed $115 to WALMART.

During the fourth month, Jason still had $445 to put toward debt. Therefore, once again, after making the combined minimum payments to the other three credit cards of $190, Jason went into WALMART and paid off the $115 balance he had with the store. The remaining

$140 from the $445 Jason put into his emergency fund, since his car had just recently begun to make some strange noises.

During the fifth month, after eliminating the WALMART credit card—thus adding an additional $15 to his disposable income—Jason now had $460 to put toward his remaining debt. Therefore, after making the combined minimum payments to the other two credit cards (VISA and MASTERCARD) of $175, Jason went into TARGET and applied the remaining $285 to his balance. Jason now only owed $185 to TARGET.

During the sixth month, Jason still had $460 to put toward debt. Therefore, once again, after making the combined minimum payments to the other two credit cards of $175, Jason went into TARGET and paid off the $185 balance. He put the remaining $100 from the $460 into his emergency fund. As a result, Jason now had $720 in his emergency fund that he could use to have his car looked at and possibly repaired. After paying off the WALMART and TARGET credit cards, Jason now had $475 he could put toward debt.

Although Jason was making progress, after six months, he finally realized he needed to find other ways to cut expenses. He was simply living beyond his means. Therefore, although Jason loved to live in the downtown area, he decided to find a less expensive place to rent in the suburbs. By doing so, Jason saved $300 per month—going from $1,200 a month in the rent he was paying to live in the downtown area to $900 a month to live in the suburbs. By finding a less expensive rental in the suburbs, Jason was now spending approximately 28 percent of his gross monthly income on housing, compared to 38 percent when he was living in downtown.

Again, through honest reflection, think about your own situation. Are there any bigger items, things, or arrangements causing you to live beyond your means? If so, could those be eliminated or could you find a less expensive alternative? Remember the long-haul perspective:

sometimes you need to sacrifice now in order to benefit later.

By Jason moving to a less expensive place, thereby saving $300 a month, in his seventh month, Jason now had $775 to put toward his debt. After making the minimum payment to his VISA credit card of $125, Jason put the remaining $650 toward his MASTERCARD debt. After making the minimum payment of $50 to MASTERCARD for the six months prior, Jason had already lowered the amount owed by $300. Therefore, Jason's starting balance of $2,000 on his MASTERCARD had been reduced by $950 by the seventh month of his plan, with $1,050 outstanding.

As you can see, by the end of the ninth month, by lowering and eliminating various fixed and variable expenses, by being disciplined (including living within his means by moving to a less expensive place), and by creating and sticking to concrete plans, Jason was able to pay off his WALMART, TARGET, and MASTERCARD credit card bills.

By doing so, Jason now had $825 to put toward his final and largest VISA credit card debt. After having paid the minimum balance of $125 for the nine months prior, amounting to $1,125, Jason still owed $3,875. However, in just five more months of paying $825 a month toward his VISA balance, Jason will be entirely debt free.

Further, after 14 months, just over a year, Jason will have an additional $950 a month at his disposal. Moreover, and even more importantly, Jason will have saved thousands of dollars in interest payments due to compound interest.

COMPOUND INTEREST: YOUR WORST ENEMY

As I mentioned above, compound interest can either be your best friend or your worst enemy. For now, let's look at how compound interest is your worst enemy, which is when it is applied to the money you owe. The term "compound interest" means that interest is charged or added to the principal, or the amount you borrowed or are borrowing by using credit. As a result, compound interest grows your debt exponentially.

For example, if you have a $100 debt and it accrues 10 percent interest every month, then in the first month, you will be charged $10 ($100 x 0.10). With compound interest, that $10 is added to your original debt, so now you have $110 of debt. The second month you are again charged 10 percent interest, but this time the interest comes to $11 ($110 x 0.10), so now you have $121 of debt. As you can see, this can add up very quickly.

Using Jason's VISA credit card balance of $5,000 as an example, since his credit score was low, due to having too many credit cards and not making minimum payments, Jason's interest rate was set at 18 percent. If he made no more purchases on his VISA credit card and only made the minimum payment of $125 every month, it would take Jason 62 months—a little over five years—to pay off this debt. Even worse is the fact that, because of compounding interest, he would have paid close to $2,700 in interest by the time his VISA debt was completely paid off. Therefore, it would be wise of Jason to both aggressively pay off his debt and learn to be more financially disciplined in order not to rack up that much debt ever again.

It is well worth your time to use an online credit card or other loan or debt interest calculator to see how much you will end up paying if you continue to pay only the minimum payments toward your debt.

COMPOUND INTEREST: YOUR BEST FRIEND

Once you have become disciplined, paid off debt, and are living within your means, it would be wise to speak with a financial advisor about how to invest your money for your future. Investing in your future needs a long-haul perspective, and it is sometimes difficult to have this long-haul perspective come into focus. In fact, one of the most challenging aspects of investing in your future is that today's money is often more valuable to us now than tomorrow's money.

For example, I remember in my beginning years of teaching, I met with a financial advisor and decided to invest $250 a month. The $250 was pretax and was automatically withdrawn from my bank account every month. Having this money automatically deposited into your investment accounts is a must, as there are far too many opportunities for you not to write that monthly check. So, no matter how you invest your money, be sure to go with the automatic direct deposit option.

Although I knew I needed to invest in my future, it felt to me that that $250 per month was worth more to me at the time—in the "now"—than the benefits I would reap 40, 50, or even 60 years later. Therefore, not being disciplined and not yet having a long-haul perspective, I stopped the automatic direct deposits after three and a half years. In hindsight, this was a huge, colossal, mammoth mistake. However, at the time, while trying to raise a family, I simply had no extra money (or at least I thought I didn't) to put toward retirement. My last deposit into that account was in 2005.

However, due to compound interest, the $10,000 I was able to invest during that time (from 2002 to 2005) was worth over $40,000 in 2017. Although I will get taxed on this money when I begin to withdraw it, since my deposits were pretax, imagine what it will be worth in 2027, 2037, and so on. Not only that, but just imagine how much more I would have in that account had I never stopped the monthly contribution of $250. I try not to think about that.

Although today's money may be more valuable to us than tomorrow's money, tomorrow's money is definitely worth more. Here, it is vital to understand that tomorrow will eventually be today. Remember that time and compound interest are your best friends when applied to the money you invest. The earlier you can start contributing the better.

Let's go back to Jason and the $950 a month at his disposal after he eliminated all of his debt. The old, undisciplined, and live-for-the-moment Jason would likely have taken that $950 a month and bought a new car, moved back to the downtown area, and started going out more. However, at just 29-years-old, the new, disciplined, and long-haul-perspective Jason now understands two of the most powerful things going for him in terms of investing his money; these are his new best friends—compound interest, and time. Therefore, even though he was offered a lot of different investment options, after speaking with a financial advisor, Jason decides to begin making contributions to a Roth individual retirement account (IRA).

A Roth IRA is a retirement account that Jason begins to automatically direct deposit funds into with his post-tax income. Roth IRAs are ideal savings vehicles for young, lower-income workers who won't miss the upfront tax deduction and will benefit from decades of tax-free, compounded growth. Also, since all Roth IRA contributions are post-tax, all future withdrawals that follow Roth IRA regulations will be tax-free. Furthermore, in case of an extreme emergency, Jason can access his contributions (but not his earnings on those contributions) at any time, tax-free and penalty-free.

Let's say that Jason chooses to contribute $400 every month for one year. After 12 months, he would have contributed $4,800. Most financial advisors you speak to will confirm that investing in a Roth IRA will yield a 6 to 8 percent return on your investment over time. Therefore, with a rate of return of 7 percent, after that first year of investment, Jason's $4,800 will have earned $336 in interest. Jason's Roth IRA would then be worth $5,136. Now let us say a real emergency comes up, and Jason needs to access some of the money in his Roth IRA. Jason would be able to access all of the $4,800 that he contributed at any time, both tax- and penalty-free, but just not the $336 that was earned from interest.

Jason will be able to access all of his money (including interest earned) when he turns 59 ½. However, the major problem with Jason prematurely withdrawing money from his Roth IRA is that the withdrawn money is no longer working for him through the mechanism of compounding interest. Thus, unless he desperately needs that money, it would be far wiser for Jason to let all the money he invested remain in his Roth IRA account, letting it grow over time, year in and year out.

Once again, speaking with a financial advisor about Roth IRAs and other savings, retirement, and investment opportunities is a cornerstone of being wise with your finances. In the meantime, there are many Roth IRA calculators on the Internet that can project how much you could earn by making regular contributions. As such, different calculators may provide slightly different amounts. With this in mind, the following table is one scenario based on a person retiring at the age of 60, an average annual rate return of 7 percent, and a yearly post-tax contribution of $4,800, or $400 per month.

Although the current maximum yearly contribution to a Roth IRA is $5,500 up until age 50—then increasing to $6,500 after age 50—I have decided to use the amount of $4,800 because many people simply may not have $5,500 to contribute every year. That said, if you can contribute $5,500, then you really ought to; it is well worth it in the end. The following table shows the incredible power of time and compound interest.

Starting Age	Principal / Contribution	Interest	Total
19	$196,800	$905,435	$1,102,235
29	$148,800	$375,447	$524,247
39	$100,800	$129,628	$230,428
49	$52,800	$28,265	$81,065

As you can see, the earlier you invest, the more time your money works for you. As another example, if an 18-year-old can begin by contributing just $600 a year to a Roth IRA—only $50 a month—until the age of 60, she could have approximately $138,000 when she reaches 60 years old. Furthermore, if you work for a company that matches employee 401(k) contributions or has other matching investment or retirement plan options, it would be well worth your time and energy to investigate this thoroughly while also speaking with a financial advisor. Then, if at all possible, begin maxing out your employer-matched contributions. This should be made a priority to succeed at your long-haul objectives.

Indeed, investing in your future is a total long-haul commitment, especially since the average life expectancy of Americans is approximately 79 years. Therefore, remember the questions from Chapter 2 when thinking about what you will be doing when you are 60–79-years-old, and beyond: Who are you with? How are you spending your time and money? Finally, how aligned are your thoughts about such questions with your current actions? Now, develop a concrete plan and get to it.

WHAT DO I NEED OR WANT TO IMPROVE?

I want to redesign the reality of my finances by contributing $X a month toward debt, and $X a month toward savings, retirement, and other investment opportunities.

WHEN WILL I DO IT?

By becoming disciplined, I will be able to put money aside for debt, savings, retirement, and other investment opportunities every month.
I will begin on this day: _____, 20_____ .

WHERE WILL I DO IT?

I will leave money in my checking or savings accounts that will be used only for bills, paying off debt, and investing in my future. By using the envelope technique, I will only take out the cash I have allotted to live off of for that month.

HOW WILL I DO IT?

First, I will determine what fixed and variable expenses I can lower or eliminate.

Second, I will learn to become disciplined and manage my day-to-day variable expenses through the envelope technique in order to save money.

Third, I will establish and begin to follow a zero-balance budget so that I can live within my means.

Fourth, I will create an emergency fund of $X.

Fifth, I will put the money saved by lowering or eliminating fixed and variable expenses toward existing debt and not toward new debt.

Sixth, after eliminating all or most debt, I will speak with a financial advisor about the best investment options for my situation and invest $X every month. I will also speak with my employer to see what retirement options they offer.

Once again, becoming disciplined and planning for your future is paramount in redesigning the reality of your finances. Therefore, no matter how much money you make, if you need assistance in creating and sticking to concrete plans in order to get out of debt, and stay out, then please visit redesignthereality.com for more information.

Finally, remember the tension discussed in Chapter 2 between planning for your future and enjoying yourself in the present moment. At some point, a good, healthy balance will need to be struck. At some point, we must learn to enjoy the journey.

CHAPTER 11: LEARN TO ENJOY THE JOURNEY

ENOUGH IS A FEAST

Many developed countries, including America, are amazing places to live. Today's modern world is a wonderful time to be alive. However, throughout time and place, there are many trappings in the world which try to rob us of our peace, joy, contentment, and money. Materialism is one such culprit.

The Buddhist saying "Enough is a feast" is countercultural to the more and more seemingly materialistic promptings of our modern world. Therefore, one day, I realized I must unplug from the debt matrix if I ever wished to live a debt-free life. Through honest reflection, I also confronted the "unconscious holdover" from my old paradigm and past mindset of constantly struggling financially, which was causing me to live only in the immediate moment, which usually meant living on credit. These actions led me to adopt the long-haul perspective.

Through the process of developing this perspective, I soon realized I had to consistently battle things that were trying to rob me of my peace, joy, contentment, and money. As I discussed in Chapters 3 and 4, I finally realized any void in my life could never be filled with "things." I had to come to a place of contentment. I finally realized that enough was truly a feast.

Therefore, however the process looks for you, and no matter how long it may take, continually try to come to a place of contentment—a state of happiness and deep satisfaction—and not be lured into the lies and deceit of materialism. Materialism lies to us by saying "just one more"—just one more purchase or upgrade will finally bring me happiness. Materialism always provides empty promises.

Every day the Internet bears witness to this reality when we see and hear of extremely wealthy people living miserable lives. Contentment, however, rests on the general premise that life is good. Of course, things could always be better, but contentment allows us to be mindful, present, and enjoy the journey as we pursue our dreams, goals, and aspirations.

MINDFULNESS

Every year, Little Italy—a neighborhood on the outskirts of downtown San Diego—hosts an Art Walk. The Art Walk is a gathering of hundreds of artists, where people stroll the streets admiring the various pieces of art and have the opportunity to meet the artists. Recently, as my wife and I were enjoying this venue, we came across the artist, McKenzie Fisk. Whenever admiring pieces of art, I enjoy reading the artist's biography and the background narrative of the piece in order to try to engage fully with what the artist was trying to portray.

Fisk's art usually features a young child interacting in some way with an animal. For example, she has an image of a little boy joyfully riding a bicycle with outstretched arms, mimicking a meandering shark adjacent to him. In another work, a little girl and a lion pridefully stand side by side with the wind blowing both the girl's hair and the lion's mane. Fisk's artwork is amazing. However, to me, what made the images particularly powerful was the reason behind her art. On her website, Fisk explains:

> I paint the fragility of the childhood experience. I use animals to best represent the agility and innocence of childhood,

an undiluted view of the world. Animals exist alongside of us, though they essentially experience life in an unadulterated way. They have no verbal language or social obligations to manipulate how they view the world around them. This perspective fascinates me. As kids, we are unencumbered by physical limitations and largely unclouded by preconceived thoughts about the world.

Most experiences are new, we lived those moments in the present, and simple things brought us the most joy. There is a purity about this time that is easily forgotten. My paintings bring us back to those times. While they represent imagined moments from my personal history, relatable childhood moments allow the viewer to enter and experience the depicted scene with memories of their own. There is no need for a verbal language to understand my work, the visual impact is a silent emotion, a feeling of peace with an understanding and mindfulness of the heart.

As Fisk portrays, both children and animals experience life in new and unadulterated ways in the now, the present. This is why trauma is so sinister; it attempts to rob children of their childhood, innocence, and peace. Unfortunately, far too many people's childhoods have not provided the opportunity for them to fully experience childhood in the way it was intended to be, namely, innocent, worry-free, and peaceful. The ACEs study discussed in Chapter 4 bears witness to this unfortunate reality.

Chronic stress and anxiety from excessive debt can also be sinister—especially to one's health and relationships—and they can rob people of their peace, joy, and contentment. When we are overwhelmed by past experiences (e.g., excessive debt) or we fret over our futures (e.g., how we are going to pay our bills), the here and now, the present moment—the only time we are truly alive—gets minimized or squeezed out. We are no longer experiencing life, but reacting to it. With this reality in mind, it will be important for people to learn to be mindful.

According to an online article in the *Greater Good Magazine*, "Mindfulness means maintaining a moment-by-moment awareness of our thoughts, feelings, bodily sensations, and surrounding environment. Mindfulness also involves acceptance, meaning that we pay attention to our thoughts and feelings without judging them—without believing, for instance, that there's a 'right' or 'wrong' way to think or feel in a given moment. When we practice mindfulness, our thoughts tune into what we're sensing in the present moment rather than rehashing the past or imagining the future."

A perfect visual for mindfulness is the "glitter in a jar" video or image. Found all over the Internet, "glitter in a jar" demonstrates what our minds look like when we are not mindful. The video or image is of a Mason jar filled with water, and with several tablespoons of glitter poured in. The jar represents our minds. The glitter represents our thoughts, worries, and anxieties.

When we are mindful, the glitter remains at the bottom so we can see clearly through the jar. However, when we are not mindful, when we are "rehashing the past or imagining the future," the jar gets tossed and turned, forcing the glitter to swirl about in the water, thus making it difficult to see through—in other words, to be mindful.

In a 2013 interview, Dr. Jon Kabat-Zinn, founder of the Mindfulness-Based Stress Reduction (MBSR) program, states, "Mindfulness is about paying attention, on purpose, in the present moment, non-judgmentally, as if your life depended on it. Attention is the faculty that allows us to navigate our lives in order to be in a wiser relationship with the things going on in our lives, rather than at the mercy of our own emotional reactions, crazy thoughts, and fears."

How many people are being tossed and turned daily by the ups and downs of life? How many people are so overwhelmed by their current financial reality that it is hard for them to see the tree of life through the forest of excessive debt? How many people are held captive by their emotional reactions, crazy thoughts, and fears, thus rendering them ineffective?

Being mindful can be powerful in slowing life down, redirecting your time and energy to what is happening in the now. By doing so, you can gain a different, and often, better perspective on what is important in life. Worry, fret, fear, and anxiety are not your friends. Peace, joy, confidence, and contentment are the platforms from which all decisions should be made, including financial ones.

With this in mind, Kabat-Zinn continues to share:

> Attending is more important than what you're attending to. With that said, if you start to pay attention to the attention we pay to anything you begin to notice that the mind is all over the place. It never sits still: this idea, and that option, and this reaction, and then we spend a huge amount of time planning and worrying about the future, and a huge amount of time reminiscing about the past.
>
> The present moment is the only time when we are ever alive in. The only time we can learn anything or express any kind of love or emotion. The only time we can be in our own body. The only time we can see, or hear, or smell, or taste, or touch, or communicate is now. Yet, the present moment gets completely squeezed out by our preoccupation with the future and the past. When we start to pay attention to our own mind and body, it is like reclaiming your life.
>
> Schools teach students how to think, but not how to be aware. Therefore, when we get into bed at the end of a long day, we cannot deal with our thoughts, and we can't sleep. We then perseverate on negative thoughts that then have the capacity to spiral us downwards.... People often take their thoughts as truth...and

end up in a very narrow band of what's actually possible for us in terms of our human experience. Mindfulness embraces the actuality of the mind, the heart, the body, and the relationality with the outside world and gives us new degrees of freedom to navigate the ups and the downs.

Thus expressed, mindfulness is not a practice, but a way of being. That said, there are practices that people can implement in order to assist themselves in being mindful, or present. If applied enough, people may begin to use such practices throughout their days, and throughout their entire lives, thereby transforming the practice into a way of being.

BEING AT PEACE

Riding on the coattails of mindfulness is the power of being at peace. However, like mindfulness, being at peace often eludes us if we concentrate too much on our current circumstances. This is where Jacuzzis come in. Being in a Jacuzzi brings me great peace, and it is often where my mind orchestrates my thoughts and surroundings to reveal all that is good in my life.

One day while on vacation in Big Bear, California, I was sitting in a Jacuzzi by myself, simply enjoying the peace and quiet of the mountains. After several minutes of soaking, a leaf drifting along the circular current of the water caught my attention. Being dried and brittle, the leaf was concave, taking on the appearance of a tiny, V-shaped coffee filter.

While observing it, I saw that the leaf encountered numerous whirlpools where it would get caught up and spin frantically for several seconds before being spewed out and sent on its way to another little whirlpool. However, after about two minutes of being tossed and turned by the various whirlpools, the leaf finally succumbed to the strength of one particular whirlpool and was sucked under the water. I watched it toss, tumble, and turn as it slowly sank.

However, once the leaf was completely under the water, it gently floated back up to the top, now upside-down, with the concave side facing the water. It was the same leaf, just reconfigured. In its new identity, the leaf drifted atop the water and resumed its circular path around the Jacuzzi, continuing to encounter the various whirlpools. This time, however, it spun only once or twice in each one before being immediately released from the whirlpools' influence, unaffected.

The reborn leaf (aka "Neo") was so unfettered by the strength of the whirlpools that a fly landed on it for refuge. At that moment, as I reflected on how my life was full of ups and downs, of tossings and turnings, I felt strongly that all was well in the world. Yet, there were people—many people, people I had never met—who had offered me refuge and provided me an environment that had allowed me to thrive.

In an online article, author Robert Emmons (2013) elaborates on finding peace and humility through gratitude in this way:

> Humility is a key to gratitude because living humbly is the truest approach to life. Humble people are grounded in the truth that they need others. We all do. We are not self-sufficient. We did not create ourselves. We depend on parents, friends, our pets, God, the universe and yes, even the government, to provide what we cannot provide for ourselves. Seeing with grateful eyes requires that we see the web of interconnection in which we alternate between being givers and receivers.
>
> The humble person says that life is a gift to be grateful for, not a right to be claimed.... Gratitude is the recognition that life owes me nothing and all the good I have is a gift.... Recognizing that everything good in life is ultimately a gift is a fundamental truth of reality. Humility makes that recognition possible. The humble

person says, "How can I not be filled with overflowing gratitude for all the good in my life that I've done nothing to merit?"

Similar to mindfulness, however, being at peace requires practice. Therefore, no matter how you practice, if being mindful and being at peace becomes a priority for you, then you should create a concrete plan on how to practice them. As an example, I provide a concrete plan for being mindful and at peace below.

WHAT DO I NEED OR WANT TO IMPROVE?

I want to make the time to become more mindful and at peace.

WHEN WILL I DO IT?

At least once a day, either in the morning, at work, or after work.

WHERE WILL I DO IT?

While at home, I will find a quiet space where I can be alone. While at work, I will shut my office door or go out to my car so that I can be alone.

HOW WILL I DO IT?

First, I will do a deep-breathing technique for two to four minutes. I will use a breathing technique where I stretch my right hand out and put my left index finger on top of my right thumb. While closing my eyes and focusing on what I am hearing and feeling physically, I will inhale deeply as my left index finger drops down my right thumb. Then, as my left index finger travels up my right index finger, I will exhale. I will do this same process for all my fingers on my right hand. If, after the two to four minutes of deep breathing, I do not feel more relaxed and present, I will repeat the process until I do.

Second, for approximately three to five minutes, I will commune with God. Through a tranquil environment provided by a more relaxed state, I will simply sit quietly with my eyes closed and meditate and soak in the presence of God.

Third, after meditating and soaking in God's presence, I will thank Him for the many blessings in my life.

By taking just eight to twelve minutes each day, I am able to renew myself by being mindful and at peace as I commune with God. At that moment, all is well in the world.

Once again, this book is not simply about assisting you in getting out of debt and being financially free; this book is also about redesigning the reality of your finances through honest reflection so that you can understand yourself, the world, and how you interact within it. As Socrates said, one must first, "Know thyself." Knowing thyself is a journey of self-discovery.

Habitsforwellbeing.com shares that part of knowing thyself is identifying and respecting—but not necessarily 100 percent accepting—your strengths and weaknesses, passions and fears, desires and dreams, thoughts and feelings, likes and dislikes, and tolerances and limitations. Once you understand yourself better, you can better understand *why* you do what you do. And, even more specifically, *why* you spend your money the way you do.

Once again, it is not enough to simply get out of debt. You must also change your mindset and systems of spending in order to avoid getting into debt again. Consequently, it is not how much money we have, necessarily, that causes us to have excessive debt, but rather, it is how we spend it and *why* we choose to do so. Many impulsive credit card purchases can probably be attributed to worry, fret, fear, and anxiety. Such things are the antithesis of peace, joy, confidence, and contentment. Therefore, as Chapter 12 will discuss, how you spend your money matters.

CHAPTER 12: HOW YOU SPEND YOUR MONEY MATTERS

SMALL THINGS ADD UP TO BIG THINGS

As previously discussed, it is not how much money we have, necessarily, that causes us to have excessive debt, but rather, how we choose to spend it. If you were like me, and constantly said, "I never have enough money," then I would like to challenge you. Through honest reflection, sit in your living room and simply take stock of everything your eyes land on. Especially if you own your home, every single thing you see probably costs you money: flooring, paint, windows, doors, appliances, and so on.

For both homeowners and renters, most everything—the television; couches; love seats; dining room table; chairs; cabinets; all the things inside the cabinets like video game systems and video games, DVDs, books, toys, and the variety of other knickknacks and gadgets—costs you money. If you would like, go into every room in your home and do this same exercise. Then, if you can bear it, go into your garage or storage unit and witness all the things your hard-earned money was spent on over the years.

Small things add up to big things. Spending $3 here and $10 there equals a lot, especially when you do not have substantial money in the bank. For example, buying a coffee or tea from Starbucks may cost you between $3 and $6 each time. If you visit Starbucks three times a week, you would be spending between $9 and $18 a week, or $36–72 a month, or $432–864 a year on beverages.

That said, please hear me: getting Starbucks is not the problem. The problem is when people spend money on things that take away from them being able to live within their means and pay off their existing debt. It is not Starbucks per se, but constant consumption—eating out on a regular basis or buying video games, DVDs, tools, gadgets, or other smaller-purchase items; these things can add up quickly. This is why, once again, until you become disciplined, you really ought to use the envelope technique discussed in Chapter 9 or another system that will keep you on top of your finances.

The following are some examples and suggestions to assist you in thinking about ways you could save money by cutting back on fixed and variable expenses, which could then be put toward eliminating debt and investing in your future. Again, everything in this book is relative, so please take the following ideas and see if they fit your situation, or feel free to brainstorm and come up with other possibilities.

EAT AT HOME

Making food at home is a great way to save money, especially when compared to going out to eat. There are many dishes that can feed a family while also providing leftovers for lunches. As one example, I make a spicy chicken sausage dish that costs around $12, feeds our family of four, and provides one day of leftovers for both my wife and me that we eat for lunch.

Here is the recipe:

INGREDIENTS:

One to three pinches of red pepper flakes (can use a package from any takeout pizza place)
One tablespoon cooking oil
3–4 garlic cloves, minced ($0.25)
One to one and a half pounds of chicken sausage, or any other

CHAPTER 12: HOW YOU SPEND YOUR MONEY MATTERS

type of sausage ($5.00)
One-pound bag of bow tie pasta, or your favorite pasta ($1.00)
One bundle of green leafy vegetables like kale, red or rainbow chard, or spinach ($2.00)
One pint of heavy whipping cream ($4.00)

Total cost for six homemade meals (four for dinner, and two for lunch leftovers): $12.25

DIRECTIONS:

Add garlic and red pepper flakes to the cooking oil.
After removing the sausage from its casing, add it to the garlic, red pepper flakes, and oil.
While frying the sausage, garlic, and red pepper flakes, boil water and cook one pound of bow tie pasta.
Once the sausage is cooked, add the heavy whipping cream and then stir.
Once the cooked sausage and heavy whipping cream are mixed, add the chopped kale, red or rainbow chard, or spinach, and let it cook down for about two minutes.
Finally, add the bow tie pasta and mix well.

This is just one example of how eating at home can save a lot of money. Now, let's look at how much feeding a family of four and one lunch for two people would cost at McDonald's.

DINNER FOR FOUR PEOPLE:

Quarter Pounder with cheese: $3.79 each x four = $15.16
Order of large french fries: $2.89 each x two (two to share) = $5.78

Total cost for dinner: $20.94

LUNCH FOR TWO PEOPLE:
Quarter Pounder with cheese: $3.79 each x two = $7.58
Order of large french fries: $2.89 each x one (one to share) = $2.89

Total cost for lunch: $10.47

Total cost for six meals from McDonald's (four for dinner, and two for lunch): $31.41

(Note: I did not include everyone getting their own french fries or drinks, which would have increased the cost considerably. Also, I did not include tax, which would have been an additional $2.51 at an 8 percent tax rate.)

Besides being healthier, the difference between six homemade meals and six McDonald's meals is $19.16 ($31.41 − $12.25 = $19.16). Netflix costs about $11 a month. By not going out to eat and making the spicy chicken sausage dish at home just one day, a family of four could save enough money to pay for Netflix for almost two months.

Furthermore, if a family of four simply reduced going out to eat at McDonald's (or any other fast-food restaurant) for six meals every week—one dinner for four people, and one lunch for two people—and ate at home instead using the spicy chicken sausage dish recipe, or a similar one, they would save $76.64 a month, or $919.68 a year. I don't know about you, but that sounds like a lot of money to me—money that could be put to much better uses.

This example is simply the difference between a homemade meal and a meal from a fast-food restaurant. Image what the difference would be if a family of four went out once a week to a nicer, sit-down restaurant.

CUT BACK WHEN EATING OUT

If you have to go out, think about not ordering soft drinks, and also sharing meals when possible. Most soft drinks cost between $1.00 and $3.00, depending on whether it is a fast-food or a sit-down restaurant. For example, if a family of four goes out to eat at a sit-down restaurant and they each order a soft drink at $2.50 each, they will end up spending $12.60 on drinks alone ($2.50 x 4 = $10.00, + 8 percent sales tax = $0.80, + 18 percent tip on $10.00 = $1.80 totals $12.60).

Once again, the $12.60 spent on soft drinks during one meal for a family meal out would have covered the cost of Netflix for a month. Of course, there are much more expensive drinks than sodas, particularly if they have alcohol. If you really want to save money, never buy alcoholic drinks at a restaurant.

Sharing meals is another great way to save money—and calories. One case in point is the time when my kids were younger and the money was tight. I always felt the need not to throw any food away when we went out to eat, so whatever was left on my kids' plates (which was usually a lot since American portions are so huge), regardless if I was still hungry or not, I would always eat it. Because of this, I was lovingly named, "The Garbage Can." It certainly wasn't long before I began to have the diameter of one.

Again, through honest reflection and confronting the "unconscious holder" from my old paradigm, what I slowly began to realize was part of my "living-for-the-moment" mentality was the need to frequently go out to eat. Upon reflection, I saw that when I did go out to eat, about halfway through my meal, I realized I was already pretty full but that I continued to eat because there was more food on my plate, and then on my kids' plates.

The nice thing about sharing meals is that when you are done eating, you can decide if you need, or even want more food. If so, simply order more. Once again, by saving the cost of a $10.00 plate of food by having two people share it, you would save an additional $12.60 (the same cost breakdown as spending money on soft drinks). Therefore, when going out to a sit-down restaurant, my family of four was able to reduce our bill by $25.20 by not ordering soft drinks and by having two of us share a meal.

Here, some people may be thinking, "Wouldn't we look cheap and offend the waitstaff if we shared a meal?" I once saw a movie that put the whole question of offending people into perspective. There is a great scene in the movie, *The Girl with the Dragon Tattoo*, that addressed this exact concern. (Mind you, there are some spoilers here, so if you have not seen it and want to, you might just skip down a couple of paragraphs.) In this particular scene, after a series of murders and the disappearance of a young lady years before, the main character, Mikael Blomkvist, an investigative journalist, finally realized who the killer was. The killer was the missing young lady's uncle, who had been helping Blomkvist with the investigation the entire time. Therefore, Blomkvist ventured to the uncle's house to snoop around.

Upon hearing the uncle come home, Blomkvist leaves the house through the back door. The uncle sees Blomkvist walking away from the house and asks him to come back inside for a drink. Having previously been friendly with each other, Blomkvist agrees. Once inside, and sensing that Blomkvist knows he is the killer, the uncle drugs Blomkvist by adding something to his drink.

As Blomkvist is feeling the effects of the drugs, the uncle reveals, "All I had to do was offer you a drink. It's hard to believe that the fear of offending can be stronger than the fear of pain. But you know what? It is." Blomkvist later wakes up in a torture chamber in the uncle's basement. If you haven't seen it, don't worry, the movie ends the way most movies do: the main character is saved, and the killer dies.

Although an extreme example, the power of the "fear of offending" should not relate to your finances. When it comes to your own, hard-earned money, do not ever be afraid of offending others. Of course, I am not talking about being rude. Rather, I am talking about not buying something because you think the salesperson might be affronted because he took so much time to help you. Or, as discussed in Chapter 9, do not be afraid to call up your credit card company and request for your interest rate be lowered. I am a firm believer in, "You don't ask. You don't get." The same principle applies when going out to eat and choosing to share a meal. No one will ever look after your best interest—and your money—better than you.

SOMETHING HAS TO GIVE

If you have numerous online subscriptions to services like Netflix, Hulu, Amazon Prime, X-Box Live, HBO, World of Warcraft, cable TV, and others, then take a hard accounting of how much time you actually spend using such products. Then compare the amounts of time and money you spend on each product to other things you enjoy doing, like going out for coffee, tea, drinks, or food, to determine which you enjoy more. Finally, be disciplined and eliminate one, two, three, or even more of the products. Or, alternatively, cut back on going out. Again, if you're living beyond your means, something has to give. So, take a hard look and then make the decision to cut back.

REUSE PREPAID CARDS THAT FIT WITHIN YOUR BUDGET

If you must go out for coffee or tea, then think about using a prepaid card. Once you have decided how much you are willing or able to spend on coffee or tea every week or month, then load that amount onto your prepaid card. Then, when it is gone, it is gone; you will not be able to buy more at your favorite place until the next week or month. This same suggestion of using a prepaid card can also be applied to going out to eat. Remember, it is all about discipline. Even better yet, make your coffee or tea at home. Then, when you do go out for it, you will savor and appreciate it all the more.

Recall the concept of hedonic adaptation from Chapter 7: hedonic adaptation can occur with both positive and negative experiences when, after repeated exposure to the same emotion-producing stimulus (e.g., Starbucks), people tend to experience less of the emotion. People get used to the bad, and to the good. Therefore, if you truly enjoy going out for coffee, tea, or food, then try limiting the number of times you go out. By doing so, you will combat hedonic adaptation, save money, and, more than likely, enjoy your coffee, tea, or meal out even more than before.

BUY WHAT YOU NEED, NOT WHAT IS ON SALE

Just because something is on sale does not mean you need it. Coupons are a great way to save money when you use them to buy things you need. However, I think far too many people use coupons to buy things they do not need simply because it seems like such a great deal. So, take inventory of what you have already in your pantry and refrigerator. Then, take the time to really think about what else you might need from the grocery store. Finally, make a list, find coupons for the items on your list, and go and buy just those items.

Remember, grocery stores put most staple foods in the back of the store, forcing you to walk through the aisles to get to them. Their hope is that you will grab some other items along the way. This is something most of us do. Therefore, do yourself and your wallet a favor and do not go grocery shopping when you are hungry. People's hunger will prompt them to buy unnecessary things that look delicious in the moment.

HAVE A CHANGE JAR FOR EXTREME CRAVINGS

Every time you come home from work or from being out, put all your change into a jar. Or, if your income allows it, along with your daily change, maybe also put in between $1.00 and $5.00 at the end of each day, or even more, depending on your income. This money then becomes a micro home savings account for you to tap into when an extreme craving overtakes you or when you need extra money for some variable expense.

For those times you are craving a coffee, tea, beer, burger, baby back ribs, or whatever else, you can tap into the jar instead of putting such things on your credit card. The amount in the jar will also dictate what you can have. As an example, if you only have $9.23, then you must find something to satisfy your craving that is $9.23 or less. That is the problem with credit cards: they allow people to overindulge on their cravings.

BUY ANNUAL PASSES

If you can afford it—and after budgeting for the expense in your zero-balance budget—purchase annual passes to local amusement parks, zoos, or other attractions that you and your family like to visit. Then, pack your own lunch and go, and enjoy yourselves on a regular basis for less money. Furthermore, if time, distance, weather, and physical ability permits, park off-site to save even more on parking. Lastly, in order to add a little variety to each excursion while also helping teach your children how to live within their means, you can allocate $X per person to spend on whatever they want while at the attraction.

As an example, the following are the costs for the San Diego Zoo annual passes compared to a one-day pass:

ANNUAL PASSES:

Two adults living in the same household: $166
One child ages 3–17 years old: $54 (x 2)

Total costs for annual passes for a family of four: $274

ONE-DAY PASSES:
One adult: $54 (x 2)
One child ages 3-17 years old: $44 (x 2)

Total costs for one-day passes for a family of four: $196

The annual passes cost an additional $78 but will provide free entry to the zoo for the entire year. Furthermore, the cost for a family of four to have annual zoo passes is approximately the same amount they would save if they opted not to order soft drinks and if two people shared one meal for 11 times of going out to eat over the course of a year ($25.20 x 11 = $277.20). Once again, it is not the amount of money you have, it's how you spend it.

My wife and I always had annual zoo passes when our kids were younger. As a family, we would pack a lunch, put it in a backpack, and then head off to the zoo. If the attraction or amusement park you are considering does not allow outside food, simply go out to your car and eat lunch there. In our case, however, the zoo did allow food. Then, because we are suckers for cheap, ballpark-style nachos, we would always supplement our homemade lunches with an order of nachos at the zoo.

Our annual zoo passes provided many great and inexpensive days of exercise, talking, and fun as we walked around the whole zoo looking at and chatting about all the different animals. Annual passes also get people up and out of the house, so they are less likely to think about some of those online subscriptions they recently canceled.

EVERYTHING HAS A COST

There is no such thing as a free lunch. Everything has a cost. For example, the stress and anxiety of the excessive debt from the new car with all the bells and whistles that a person buys with money they do not have can easily rob them of their peace. Therefore, it is highly suggested that you begin to buy things you can afford, and not things where only the minimum payments fit into your monthly budget.

I believe far too many people buy things based on minimum payments. Consequently, they throw thousands of dollars away in interest while also leaving little to no room for error in their budgets (if they even have or follow one) due to the litany of "things" they bought.

For instance, when buying a car, if you do not need—let alone, cannot afford—leather seats and a higher quality sound system, to name just two items, then do not get them. Simply look for and purchase a car that will do its job: safely and economically get you from point A to point B. If you think owning a pedestrian and economical car is not good enough, then ask yourself, "*Why*?"—especially if you are considering buying something you really cannot afford.

What need or void are you trying to fill by buying an expensive car with all the bells and whistles? There are reasons why purchasing a car is a highly emotional event and associated with high-pressure tactics. Thus, do not fall into the trappings of buying all the bells and whistles that are offered with a new car purchase. Remember, little things add up to big things.

Let's say that after creating and following a zero-balance budget, you are somewhat disciplined and begin looking for a new car that is economical. Nothing fancy, just something to safely get you from point A to point B. Now, let's say you actually find the car at the right price and walk into the dealership to buy it. However, during the various negotiations with the salesperson, he is able to convince you to upgrade to leather seats and exchange the stock sound system for a higher quality one. The salesperson tells you that these two upgrades will only cost an additional $1,500, but will also increase the resale value of the car in case you ever want to sell it. Not only that, but you do not want to offend the salesperson, who has been so kind and who has spent so much time helping you, so you agree with him when he says, "You work hard. You deserve to ride in style!"

Continuing this scenario, let's say that since you are still recovering from past unwise spending practices, you have a low credit score and no money for a down payment. The salesperson says it's "no problem," but gives you a higher interest rate of 15 percent. Therefore, the terms of the loan—the principal—including the upgrades, is $16,000 for the car, with a 15 percent interest rate, for 60 months (or five years), equaling a monthly payment of approximately $381. If you only make the minimum payment each month, after five years, you will have paid $6,838 in interest, thus bringing the total price of the car to $22,838.

Now, let's say you were disciplined and not afraid of offending the salesperson, so you decided not to get the upgrades. As a result, you only financed $14,500 (instead of $16,000). Your monthly payment would drop to $345 a month, putting $36 back into your pocket each month that you could apply to the principal, and by the time you pay off the car, you will have saved $641 in interest over the five years. If you simply chose not to get the upgrades, you would have saved $2,141 ($1,500 + $641 = $2,141).

Now, let's look at this example using the long-haul perspective and revisit how time and compounding interest are your best friends when it comes to investing money. Let's say you are 29 years old. Therefore, you take the saved $2,141 and put it into a Roth IRA account. With an average rate of return of 7 percent, that $2,141 would earn you an additional $15,298 in compounding interest, turning your original investment of $2,141 into $17,439 by the time you turn 60 years old. Therefore, in a different reality, those $1,500 upgrades could actually end up costing you $17,439 or more over your lifetime. Although one might think this is an extreme example, the numbers don't lie. Once again, it is not how much money you have, but how you spend it that matters most.

Therefore, whether it is a new car, new clothes, new appliances, or any other type of purchase, do not add on unnecessary bells and whistles to the principal or the final cost. More importantly, if you cannot pay cash and have to finance something, do not budget that purchase based on the minimum payments. Rather, budget and plan to pay off interest-accruing purchases as soon as you can in order to avoid paying too much in interest.

For example, for the first monthly payment of $381 on the $16,000 car loan, $200 of the $381 would go to interest, and only $181 would go to the principal. After the first year, or after the twelfth payment, you would have paid $4,572 ($381 x 12 = $4,572). Of that $4,572, $2,247 would have gone to interest and only $2,325 would have gone to the principal. Further down the road, by the beginning of the fourth year, or the forty-eighth payment, the amount going to interest would have decreased to $57, and the amount toward principal would have increased to $324.

After that first year of payments, the $2,247 you paid in interest would have been 33 percent of the total amount of interest for the five-year loan ($2,247 / $6,838 of total interest = 33 percent). This is how financing companies make their money: more interest is charged at the beginning of a loan, before people have the time, money, or opportunity to pay it all back.

Therefore, before making a purchase on credit, it is well worth your time to go online and plug your loan numbers into an amortization calculator in order to see how much you will be paying in interest over the lifetime of the loan. Hopefully, by seeing the amounts you will pay toward interest will encourage you to borrow less—or perhaps nothing at all—and pay far more each month than the minimum payment.

One final thought related to the "everything has a cost" suggestion. If you find that it is difficult to live within your means because your means are too low, that you simply do not earn enough money, and you do not have a college degree or some type of advanced training or certified trade or skill, then you should reread Chapters 5 and 6 and not finance a new car or take out a loan for any substantial amount of money until you graduate from college or obtain education in a trade. I have heard about far too many people dropping out of school because they could not afford to both go to school and make the payments on a new car they had recently financed. Unfortunately, these people did not have the long-haul perspective. They wanted to enjoy life in the moment, not realizing the price it would cost them in the future.

With only a minimum-wage job, most car dealerships are more than happy to "work with you" in order to get you into that new car with all the bells and whistle that you can only "afford" through financing. However, with low or bad credit, your interest rate will be much higher. Consequently, your monthly payment and the amount you will have paid in interest will also be much higher. Ultimately, people's decision to drop out of school to pay for a new car could cost them hundreds of thousands of dollars in earning potential over their lifetimes. Everything has a cost.

GO ON MICRO ADVENTURES

A micro adventure is usually a one-day experience that you can do in the general area where you live. For instance, when my kids were younger, we would all go on "trolley adventures." Since kids were free on the weekend with a paid adult, my wife and I would buy two $5 day passes, pack sandwiches and snacks, and jump on the trolley with the kids for a day full of jumping on and off the trolley in different parts of San Diego.

Then, once again, if we had budgeted the money, we would stop for a movie, or dinner, or both. If we did not have the money, we would simply walk, talk, and enjoy the sights and each other's company. Honestly, our "trolley adventures" created many awesome memories, sometimes only costing $10 for the entire day.

Another simple micro adventure is going on walks, or as I call them, "lovers' walks"—something that always made my kids want to vomit when I said my wife and I were going to take one. Lovers' walks are where you simply take a walk with your spouse or significant other to a place and get something to eat or drink. By walking, you are exercising, being outside, and taking yourself away from the need to want to access all those online subscriptions you have just eliminated. Just as importantly, they also provide ample opportunity for you and your significant other to converse.

If you want to save even more money, then only take a certain pre-agreed amount and find a place during your walk where you can purchase something for that amount. On our lovers' walks, my wife and I always share a meal and a vanilla latte with whole milk. By doing so, we can experience two different days of meals and lattes for the price of one had we each gotten them on our own. Once disciplined, micro adventures do not need to be expensive.

If you have children, then go on family walks and do the same thing. Depending on the ages of your children, you could also teach them about living within their means by giving them their own money during the walk and allowing them to decide how they are going to spend it. Even more powerful is when you tell them you will be making several stops at different places, so they will need to make sure to budget their money wisely.

The whole point of a micro adventure is to get out of the house, experience the world around you, and—by doing so—realize how much you have to be grateful for.

CHAPTER 13: GRATITUDE

FOREVER GRATEFUL

Through much reflection and research, I have come to the conclusion that—first and foremost—operating out of a place of gratitude is at the core of a person becoming the best, healthiest version of themselves. Therefore, I have decided to end with gratitude. By doing so, I hope you will be able to sit back, reflect on your life, and truly see that life is good.

An education opens doors, broadens horizons, and fosters dreams of what could be. America is an incredible country that understands and values the importance of education. By providing free, comprehensive, kindergarten through high school education for all of its citizens, America not only establishes a strong foundation for the country but also provides opportunities for individuals to create strong foundations for themselves and their families. However, this is not the case worldwide.

If at all possible, I believe every person should go on a two- to four-week trip to a developing country sometime in their life. Not entirely their fault, necessarily, but many people take for granted all the opportunities afforded to them simply by living in the United States. I know I did, and, on occasion, still do. However, what really opened my eyes to all the opportunities America affords me was when my wife and I went to Swaziland, Africa.

One Sunday while in church, an organization called Dream for

Africa spoke about the dire situations that many people living in Africa faced. The premise was that some people's diets were so poor that their bodies could not receive immunizations or certain kinds of medical treatment, let alone being able to properly fuel and support their bodies. Dream for Africa asked for volunteers to travel to Swaziland and plant gardens for local people so they could supplement their diets through the renewable food source of gardens. Both my wife and I felt compelled to go.

At the time, I was a high school social science teacher, and I spoke with my principal regarding Dream for Africa. I asked if I could approach the students and staff about partnering with my wife and me through donations since the cost to make the trip was $3,000 per person. After researching other needs that people in Africa had that I felt we could assist with, I decided to ask the students and staff for shoe donations as well.

I visited various classrooms and presented a talk on what I was doing and why. By the end, the students and staff had donated over $3,300 and 180 gently-worn pairs of shoes. Even though the students and staff were not going to Africa, they believed in the cause and trusted me, so they gave generously. Finally, my wife and I were off to Swaziland with three, four-foot long duffle bags stuffed with 180 pairs of shoes, as well as a strong sense of purpose to help those who were less-fortunate than ourselves.

After 48 hours of travel, (including being on the airplane for 20 hours straight), we finally arrived in Swaziland. We were there for seven days, and every day we would be driven one to two hours away from the hotel and dropped off to walk to various homesteads with seedlings to plant. In addition to the seedlings, we also carried dozens of pairs of shoes with us daily to distribute to the homesteads. As one could image, the conditions the people lived in were startling.

Although we visited many homesteads, to this day, I still hold the memory of a particular one in my heart. We were at the end of our day and had already depleted our supply of shoes for that particular day. As we approached the last homestead, five children came running up to meet us, since word had gotten out that we were planting gardens. After we finished and were talking with the family, I could not help but notice how ragged the man's clothes were and how he was not wearing shoes. Having brought an extra pair of clothes and a pair of sandals for the ride home, I dropped my bag, took out the clothes, and began taking off my shoes to give to him.

Watching me, the man fell to his knees, tears running down his face, and arms reaching up to the sky. I have never felt so ashamed. Here was a man, the same age as myself, being so incredibly thankful to receive a used pair of pants, a shirt, and a pair of shoes. The man finally rose to his feet and embraced both me and his new clothing.

On the bus ride back to Johannesburg International Airport, I was reflecting on everything I had just experienced, particularly the extreme poverty and absolute lack of what so many people—including myself—take for granted on a daily basis: running water, food in the pantry, choices, and opportunities. There was so much need that I found myself asking God, "Why did I come here? What was I supposed to see, learn, or do?" The response I felt deep within myself was God gently saying, "Marc, most people here will never have the chance to have what you have. No matter how intelligent or hardworking they are, they do not have the opportunities to get out of the situations they are in." I then reflected further: How much of what I have and have accomplished is due to my hard work and abilities, and how much is truly related to the opportunities that have been afforded to me by so many other people's sacrifices?

Upon our return (and long before Facebook and other social media platforms existed), I created a slide show using the pictures my wife and I took in order to show the students and staff our experiences, as, of course, they, too, were an integral part of our journey, giving us the ability to go. I'll never forget one teacher telling me how excited a student was after viewing the slide show and seeing a Swazi man wearing the pair of shoes he had donated. Although the student could not go on the trip, he felt very good because he took advantage of the opportunity to give.

THE POWER OF GRATITUDE

Having studied appreciation and gratefulness for over a decade, Robert Emmons (2010), a professor of psychology at the University of California, Davis, identifies two crucial components of gratitude: 1) an affirmation of goodness—that there are good things in the world, gifts, and benefits we have received; and 2) figuring out where that goodness comes from, and recognizing the sources of that goodness is outside of ourselves. True gratitude involves a humble dependence on other people, and sometimes a higher power, who gave us the many gifts that have helped us achieve the goodness in our lives.

Kerry Howells (2012) provides a powerful example of Emmons's description of gratitude when she discusses having gratitude "for" water, which leads to showing gratitude "to" people and things:

> When we stand under the shower we can think of how wonderful it is to have water, to feel gratitude for all the things that have brought this water to us, where the water comes from, and all the efforts of both nature and humans to warm the water. Perhaps this could extend to our loved ones and our homes and those who have provided us with our material blessings. This would be a way of awakening our gratitude. When we move to expressing gratitude for water, by trying to preserve it and having a shorter shower, it becomes gratitude in the truer sense of the word. (p. 48)

Howells also provides distinctions between gratitude "for" and gratitude "to," writing that gratitude "for" is the basis of being grateful "to" (p. 37):

- Gratitude "for": internalized, emotion, receiving, self, solipsistic, materialistic, therapy

- Gratitude "to": externalized, action, giving, other, altruistic, transcendent, transformational

With the above distinctions in mind, and expressing that, "Complexities lie in the need to have a definition of gratitude that respects difference, is suitable to the modern day, is secular, is adaptable to students and teachers, but is not confused with other concepts" (p. 37), Howells provides a definition of gratitude as something that "goes beyond an emotion or thought to be something that is actualized in one's daily life through the heartfelt active practice of giving thanks. Gratitude is usually expressed toward someone or something. It is also an inner attitude that can be understood as the opposite of resentment or complaint" (pp. 37–38). Therefore, being grateful requires action.

For me, my experience in Swaziland, Africa, and of the man's embrace, tears, and thankfulness for the shoes and clothing personified Emmons's and Howells's definitions of gratitude. The experience made me realize I had things—good things—in my life that I did not earn. I simply received them: love, health, freedom, and opportunity. Even though there are times when I have my own private "pity parties"—which is okay, by the way, since we do not have to be, nor is it possible to be grateful 100 percent of the time—I have tried, throughout my life, to make a conscious effort to keep things in perspective and appreciate all the blessings in my life, and to be thankful to those who have sacrificed in order to provide me incredible opportunities.

BENEFITS OF GRATITUDE

The University of California, Berkeley's "Greater Good in Action: Science-Based Practices for a Meaningful Life" provides a list of the social, physical, and psychological benefits of gratitude, compiled over the past decade through hundreds of studies. As you will see, the benefits of gratitude can actually assist in filling the void that many people have in their lives. By identifying and affirming all the good, people are able to focus more on what they have, and less on what they do not have.

By doing so, people not only appreciate—and show appreciation for and to—all the people and things in their lives but, hopefully, also come to a place of contentment where "enough" is truly a feast. When enough becomes a feast, the voids in people's lives no longer need to be filled with "things." Consequently, money saved from buying such "things" can then be used for eliminating debt, investing in their futures, and becoming financially free.

GRATITUDE BRINGS US HAPPINESS:

Practicing gratitude has been proven to be one of the most reliable methods for increasing happiness and life satisfaction. It also boosts feelings of optimism, joy, pleasure, enthusiasm, and other positive emotions. Gratitude also reduces anxiety and the frequency and duration of episodes of depression.

GRATITUDE IS GOOD FOR OUR BODIES:

Gratitude strengthens the immune system, lowers blood pressure, reduces symptoms of illness, and makes us less bothered by aches and pains. It also encourages us to exercise more and take better care of our health.

GRATEFUL PEOPLE ARE MORE STRESS RESISTANT AND RESILIENT:

Research suggests that people with a grateful disposition recover more quickly from serious trauma, adversity, and suffering. Emmons (2010) states, "Gratitude gives people a perspective from which they can interpret negative life events and help them guard against post-traumatic stress and lasting anxiety." This sounds a lot like the definition of "wisdom" found in Chapter 3; that through knowledge, experience, and deep understanding, wisdom is facing life's uncertainties with calm optimism.

GRATEFUL PEOPLE SLEEP BETTER:

Those who are grateful get more hours of sleep each night, spend less time awake before falling asleep, and feel more refreshed upon waking up. Therefore, if you want to sleep more soundly, count blessings, not sheep.

GRATITUDE STRENGTHENS RELATIONSHIPS:

Gratitude makes people feel closer and more committed to their friends and romantic partners. When partners feel and express gratitude for each other, they each become more satisfied with their relationship. Gratitude may also encourage a more equitable division of labor between partners.

GRATITUDE BLOCKS TOXIC, NEGATIVE EMOTIONS:

Emotions such as envy, resentment, and regret can destroy our happiness. People cannot feel envy or resentment and gratitude at the same time. They are incompatible feelings.

While I was presenting a talk on trauma-informed care to a group of high school teachers, one participant shared that when she had feelings of animosity toward her ex-husband, she would intentionally turn the resentment she felt into a feeling of gratitude by saying to herself, "Thank you, John. If it were not for you, I would not have my son, Timmy." Since resentment and gratitude are opposing feelings, a person cannot experience one while simultaneously experiencing the other. Thus, by intentionally practicing gratitude, this woman was able to experience less and less resentment toward her ex-husband.

GRATITUDE PROMOTES FORGIVENESS:
The 1996 book, *Into the Wild*, by Jon Krakauer, which was later made into a movie, chronicles Christopher McCandless's journey of both self-discovery and the search for truth. Being hurt by his family's dysfunction, McCandless abandons all his possessions after graduating from Emory University and begins a hitchhiking journey to the Alaskan wilderness.

Along the way, McCandless encounters several important characters who help shape his life. One such person is 80-year-old Ronald Franz. In the part of the movie titled, "The Getting of Wisdom," Franz, seeing the pain in McCandless's life, offers a piece of wisdom that could only be gained through the life experience of sharing it: "When you forgive, you love. And when you love, God's light shines upon you."

In agreement with this notion, Adam Sáenz (2012) shares that forgiveness is good and healthy for people, as research has identified several key adaptive, quality-of-life characteristics in individuals who practice forgiveness: empathy, emotional intelligence, life satisfaction, and spiritual well-being.

Conversely, research has linked unforgiveness with a wide range of mental and physical disorders, including depression, anxiety, eating disorders, nicotine dependence, headaches, and physical tension. According to Sáenz, clinging to unforgiveness inevitably damages you far more than it punishes the offending party (p. 59). Or, as Nelson Mandela once said, "Resentment is like drinking poison and then hoping it will kill your enemies."

GRATITUDE ENCOURAGES PEOPLE TO "PAY IT FORWARD":
Grateful people are more helpful, altruistic, and compassionate. I experienced this benefit of gratitude while at Balboa Park—an amazingly beautiful park bordering downtown San Diego. Every year Balboa Park hosts an event called "December Nights," a gathering of diverse food and people to celebrate the holiday season. On one annual visit to "December Nights," my wife and I were taking a lovers' walk through the park, soaking in the sights, sounds, and smells. As we were strolling, I noticed a young male caregiver assisting an extremely disabled young man. The disabled man was in a wheelchair that allowed him to be almost horizontal in order to accommodate his seemingly perpetual convulsing body. It was clear that he was unable to control any part of his body. The caregiver was 100 percent attentive to the man's needs, constantly and carefully wiping the man's face, and readjusting him in the wheelchair, so that he would be more comfortable.

As I watched this beautiful example of compassionate care, an extreme sense of gratitude came over me. I was grateful for people like the caregiver, who devoted himself to serving the extreme needs of another human being. Then, deep inside of me, I felt the need to express this gratitude to him. I walked up to the young caregiver and said, "As I was watching you care for this young man, I could not help but sense that God sees you and is extremely proud of you. What you are doing is truly amazing. I just wanted to let you know that you are known, cared for, and very much respected and appreciated." I then handed him $5 and said, "I know it is not a lot, but I would love for you to buy yourself something to eat on me."

Without being aware, right behind me, another man had been listening to our conversation and said, "I couldn't agree more with what he just said," and handed the young caregiver $20. At that moment, the young caregiver began to weep and threw his arms around me. As we hugged, I said to him, "You're a good man."

Part of "paying it forward" is being generous with your time, talent, and treasures. Although it may not feel like it, no matter how difficult your current situation is, there is always someone else who is worse off. Therefore, I am a firm believer in being generous. Being generous not only blesses another person, but it also blesses you. I cannot explain how it works, but I truly believe that when you give, you also receive in ways you may never fully know or understand.

Therefore, no matter how much treasure (i.e., money) people have, we all have time and talent—and even a little bit of treasure—to do something nice for another person. There was much truth when Mark Twain remarked, "The best way to cheer yourself up is to try to cheer somebody else up."

Finally, you are not asked to help every person in need you encounter. That burden is not yours to carry. However, when an opportunity presents itself, remember love is a verb. *Love does.*

WHY PRACTICING GRATITUDE IS IMPORTANT

We have all heard the saying, "The grass is always greener on the other side of the fence," and understand that it refers to the way people tend to look at other people's lives through rose-colored glasses, ignoring anything negative about the other person and downplaying everything positive about themselves. It is refreshing that both wisdom and research provides an answer to the universal dilemma of covetousness, and the act of comparing our Monday-through-Friday lives to other people's highlight reels.

Consequently, gratitude becomes the flaming dagger that pierces the cold heart of discontentment, resentment, and the mundane. As the writer William Arthur Ward professes, "Gratitude can transform common days into thanksgivings, turn routine jobs into joy, and change ordinary opportunities into blessings. Feeling gratitude and not expressing it is like wrapping a present and not giving it."

Emmons (2010) shares that our emotional system craves newness, novelty, and change, which thus results in positive emotions quickly wearing off. Basically, people adapt to positive life circumstances; things that were once new and exciting eventually become familiar and mundane. Hence, the grass you planted last year is nothing compared to your neighbor's freshly planted, greener grass.

The same can hold true regarding buying a new car or house, getting a new job, or even getting a new spouse. As discussed in Chapter 6, this adaptation to the familiar is what psychologists termed hedonic adaptation. In simple terms, similar to experiencing consistently bad situations that people then become used to, people can also quickly take for granted the things that made them happy.

Therefore, in order to more fully appreciate the good things in our lives, we need to intentionally practice gratitude by constantly examining what we are thankful for, who we are thankful to, and why. In the act of doing so, we will become happier people. Consequently, as expressed on happierhuman.com, "It is a psychological imperative to fight hedonic adaptation if we want to maximize happiness. Gratitude is one of the most powerful tools in our arsenal." The core of gratitude is that it allows us to celebrate the good in our lives in the present moment. Gratitude magnifies positive emotions, and so doing, assists us in appreciating the value of things on a daily basis. Emmons (2010) explains, "When we appreciate the value of something, we extract more benefits from it; we're less likely to take it for granted. In effect, gratitude allows us to participate more in life. We notice the positives more, and that magnifies the pleasures you get from life. Instead of adapting to goodness, we celebrate goodness" (p. 3).

The following parable of the monk, the tigers, and the blackberry bush illustrates the importance of celebrating the present and being grateful both for and to the people and things right in front of us.

> *Once upon a time, a monk was walking deep in thought through a forest. Suddenly, a huge tiger jumped out from the bushes. Frightened, the monk ran. Rapidly, the tiger was at the monk's heels when the monk tumbled over a cliff. As he rolled down the cliff, he caught hold of a wild blackberry bush. Dangling from the bush, the monk's hands began to hurt from its thorns. Just as he was about to drop down to the bottom of the cliff, a second tiger appeared below, clearly lying in wait. The monk did not know what to do. Looking at the blackberry bush, the monk noticed the bush had a lone berry on it. Picking the berry, he ate it. It was the best berry he had ever eaten.*

The power of this parable is that there are many ways to interpret it. However, in relation to gratitude, what does the blackberry represent to you? It may be something you have experienced many times before, but haven't fully appreciated, at least not recently. Is it your spouse or significant other? Your children or grandchildren? Your home, job, or finances? Your health? Your freedom, rights, or opportunities?

Not wanting to wait until we are in a life-or-death situation to become fully aware of who or what we are grateful for or to, the final chapter of this book is intended to assist people in practicing gratitude on a regular basis. The grass is never greener on the other side of the fence. The grass is only greener where you water it.

INTENTIONALLY CULTIVATING GRATITUDE

Although not a giant, at 6-foot-3 and weighing 215 pounds, I am a pretty big guy. I have good, strong genes, which have provided me a strong frame. However, for many different reasons, I abhor working out (except for taking long walks), so my body is not in the shape I know it could be. Since muscle has memory, when I do work out, my arms remember the days of being a busboy and all the heavy lifting I once did.

Once, within a matter of few days of working out, my biceps and triceps became much more muscular and defined than my chest. Although my genes have afforded me a muscular frame—something I am grateful for, since I did nothing to acquire it—it still takes effort on my part to develop that frame, with some parts of my body requiring much more intentional focus than others.

As the scholar Jane Wilson (2016) reveals, research finds that the same can be said about gratitude:

> Researchers have investigated whether gratitude is a genetic disposition or learned trait. Lyubomirsky, Sheldon, and Schkade (2005) argue that 50% of one's tendency toward happiness is related to one's genetic set point, 10% to circumstance, and 40% to intentional activity. Psychologists have identified a group of intentional activities, called 'gratitude practices,' that can be used to strengthen one's level of happiness or gratitude.
>
> When people intentionally chose to engage in gratitude practices, researchers have found that practitioners experienced an overall enhanced sense of well-being (Emmons & McCoullough, 2003). Though gratitude might not come naturally to some people, it can be learned with a certain level of introspection and reflection (Froh, Miller, and Snyder, 2007). For example, researchers found that participants who daily recounted blessings were training their brains with cognitive habits which amplified the good in their lives (Watkins et al., 2014). It appears that gratitude can be cultivated with intentional practice. (pp. 2–3)

Basically, then, through intentional practice (i.e., through "Not Yet"

Practices), we can all learn to be more grateful.

However, practicing gratitude intentionally is similar to when people decide to take better care of themselves by exercising and eating healthier...again. I am sure this is how many companies make so much money, especially gyms. People get "motivated," temporarily; they go out and buy workout apparel and shoes, exercise equipment, or gym memberships. Then, in a matter of months, or sometimes just weeks, many people's drive diminishes with the omnipresent feeling of failure lurking in the backdrop. Finally, as life can do, being tossed and turned in the sea of overwhelmingness, people retreat back to what they know: the comfort of predictability, which often leads to the mundane. The status quo is resurrected. This often happens when people "fall off the wagon" when trying to eat better, or when they try to cut back on spending money.

Many people end up reasoning, "What's the use? I might as well just enjoy life and eat and buy what I want, when I want it," instead of acknowledging that they simply stumbled—that it is not the end of their attempt at trying; rather, they must merely recommit to their plan. However, I think this is the problem for many of us: we do not have a concrete plan in place from the beginning.

Recall Carol Dweck's (2006) sage advice from Chapter 8: "When people drop the good-bad, strong-weak thinking that grows out of the fixed mindset, they're better able to learn useful strategies that help with self-control. Every lapse doesn't spell doom. It's like anything else in the growth mindset. It's a reminder that you're an unfinished human being and a clue to how to do it better next time" (p. 242).

Once again, this is why "Not Yet" Practices—whether related to your finances, health, practicing gratitude, or in any other area of your life—need to be anchored in concrete plans. With this in mind, this book's final chapter provides gratitude practices that have been proven to yield positive benefits, but only when applied and practiced.

CHAPTER 14: PRACTICE GRATITUDE

A SURREAL MOMENT

During my 22 years in public education, I have seen, unfortunately, plenty of knives, and even several guns, but never a hand grenade. Until that one day...

"Mr. Barlow! I just saw a student throw this into the trash can!" exclaimed a student as he ran toward me with a hand grenade in his hand. With students everywhere—it was lunchtime in a high school of over 1,700 students—the first and only question that came racing to my mind was, "How long have you had this?!" Hand grenades have a very specific timeline.

Grabbing the grenade from his hand, I quickly surveyed my surroundings and noticed a large boulder adjacent to a stand-alone, portable classroom. As fast as I could, I ran up the slightly inclined hill and threw the hand grenade in between the boulder and the classroom. I then bolted into the classroom and evacuated the teacher and the several students who were with her. Finally, I called in the situation to the other administrators, campus security, and the school resource officer. The school immediately went into lockdown. It was surreal.

Within minutes, multiple law enforcement officers were on campus with a bomb squad on the way. About 30 minutes after the incident, law enforcement was able to identify the hand grenade as being inert. Although the grenade was real, the explosive materials inside had been removed. The inert hand grenade had been a gift to the student who had thrown it into the trash can.

Although there was a whole backstory as to why the student brought the hand grenade to school, causing this whole incident to occur, since the student involved was severely mentally disabled, I have decided not to share those details. Let's just say that at that moment when the hand grenade was presented to me, I didn't care why or how it got there.

Although nothing tragic happened—thank God!—after experiencing such an event, your mind instantly goes to the ones you love and how thankful you are to be alive. Your mind does not go to all the "things" you have accumulated. Unfortunately, far too many people wait much too long to truly express how grateful they are for and to the people in their lives. In the end, people do not long to be surrounded by their "things." Instead, they want to be surrounded by those whom they love.

Therefore, if you take nothing else away from this book, take this: appreciate those closest to you, and practice telling them how grateful you are for and to them on a regular basis. Let them know you love them. Yes, money is important; however, money is only a vehicle to the life experiences that you either need or want. Your loved ones, and your relationships with them, is what truly makes the journey of life worth living. Recall the book and movie, *Into the Wild*, discussed in Chapter 13. Dying alone in the Alaskan wilderness, Christopher McCandless finally realized—on one of his last days on earth—a profound truth: "Happiness is only real when shared."

GUIDELINES TO INTENTIONALLY CULTIVATE GRATITUDE

Based on recent studies, there are numerous behaviors and practices—ranging from general to specific—that can increase people's sense of gratitude.

Generally speaking, it appears that grateful people have a particular linguistic style to describe the good in their lives, using words such as gifts, givers, blessings, blessed, fortune, fortunate, and abundance (Emmons, 2010). For instance, in referring to their job, a grateful person might say, "My job is such a blessing." By doing so, the person is valuing the fact that their job is the culmination of many different people's efforts and contributions to their life: their parents, their significant other, their teachers and bosses, and even a higher power. Other behavioral attributes of grateful people include smiling, saying "thank you," and writing letters of gratitude—things Emmons refers to as "grateful motions," which will, ultimately, trigger gratitude.

Recall from Chapter 13 the researchers that state that only 50 percent of a person's happiness is related to his or her genetics, with the other 10 and 40 percent related to circumstance and intentional activity, respectively. From this, we understand that happiness can be influenced by outside factors. In fact, from their work, we see that 40 percent of your happiness can be controlled by you through intentional activities—activities like practicing gratitude.

With this reality in mind, it is important for people to reflect on their inner condition on a daily basis—the concealed lens they look through that influences their thoughts, feelings, words, self-talk, attitudes, behaviors, and actions (Howells, 2012). Remember, right thinking is the raw material for right actions. People's actions will naturally reveal the direction of their thoughts. Therefore, it is important that you take the time to think about and acknowledge all the good in your life.

KEEP A GRATITUDE JOURNAL OR WRITE ABOUT THREE GOOD THINGS

The University of California, Berkeley's "Greater Good in Action: Science-based Practices for a Meaningful Life," suggests writing in a gratitude journal or, even more simply, writing about three good things that happened during the week.

So, once or twice a week, write down three to five things or specific blessings for which you feel grateful. The physical record is important—don't just do this exercise in your head. The things you list can be relatively small in importance (e.g., "the tasty sandwich I had for lunch today") or relatively large (e.g., "my sister gave birth to a healthy baby boy"). The goal of the exercise is to remember a good event, experience, person, or thing in your life. Then, sit and enjoy the good emotions that come with it.

As suggested by Berkeley's "Greater Good in Action," as you write, try to keep the following tips in mind:

- Be as specific as possible. Specificity is key to fostering gratitude. For example, "I am grateful that my coworkers brought me soup when I was sick on Tuesday" will be more effective than "I'm grateful for my coworkers."

- Go for depth over breadth. Elaborating in detail about a particular person or thing for which you are grateful carries more benefits than a superficial list of many things.

- Get personal. Focusing on people to whom you are grateful has more of an impact than focusing on things for which you are grateful.

- Try subtraction, not just addition. Consider what your life would be like without certain people or things, rather than just tallying up all the good stuff. Be grateful for the negative outcomes you avoided, escaped, or prevented, or those negative things you turned into something positive.

- See good things as "gifts." To avoid hedonic adaptation, think of the good things in your life as gifts to guard against taking them for granted.

- Savor surprises. Try to record events that were unexpected or surprising, as these tend to elicit stronger levels of gratitude.

- Revise if you repeat. It is okay to write about the same people and things. However, try to zero in on a different aspect in detail in each remembrance.

- Write consistently. Create a concrete plan as to when and where to journal; then follow through.

- Don't overdo it. Evidence suggests that writing occasionally (1–3 times per week) is more beneficial than daily journaling. Again, hedonic adaptation may cause us to adapt to positive events, thereby causing us to become numb to them eventually.

GRATITUDE LETTER (OR EMAIL)

Call to mind someone who did something for you for which you are extremely grateful, but to whom you never expressed your deep gratitude. This could be a relative, friend, teacher, colleague, or co-worker. Describe in specific terms what this person did, why you are grateful to them, and how the person's behavior positively affected your life. Try to be as concrete as possible. Describe what you are doing in your life now and how you often remember her or his efforts. Then, either mail the letter, hit "send," or have a face-to-face conversation with that person where you either hand them the letter or read it to them.

Wilson (2016) finds, "In this gratitude practice [gratitude letter], one selects an individual whom he or she has never properly thanked and then writes that person a letter (approximately 300 words) that expresses specific thanks. Research suggests that writing, delivering, and receiving a gratitude letter can enhance joy for both the author and the receiver (Froh, Kashdan, Ozimkowski, & Miller, 2009: Seligman et al., 2005)" (p. 3).

MENTAL SUBTRACTION OF RELATIONSHIPS

Again, as suggested by Berkeley's "Greater Good in Action," take a moment to think about an important relationship in your life. Think back to where and how you met this person. Consider the ways in which you might never have met this person and never formed a relationship, for instance, if you had not decided to go to a certain party, taken a certain class, or moved to a certain city.

Write down all of the possible events and decisions—large and small—that could have gone differently and prevented you from meeting this person. Imagine what your life would be like now if events had unfolded differently and you had never met them. Bring to mind some of the joys you have enjoyed as a result of your relationship with them. Then, consider how you would feel if you were denied all those specific joys.

Next, shift your focus to remind yourself that you did actually meet this person, and reflect on the benefits that the relationship has brought you. Finally, allow yourself to feel grateful that things happened as they did and this person is in your life.

Try to make time to do this practice several times a month, focusing on a different person each time. It might help to do this practice at the same time, for example, before bed on Sunday evenings or during lunch on Fridays.

SAVORING WALKS WITH GRATITUDE CONVERSATIONS

And again, as suggested by Berkeley's "Greater Good in Action," set aside 20–30 minutes several times a week to take a walk outside by yourself or with a loved one. As you walk, try to notice as many positive things around you as you can. These can be sights, sounds, smells, or other sensations. For instance, you could focus on the breathtaking height of a tree, the intricate architecture of a building, a child playing with a puppy, the sun setting or rising, the smell of the grass or of flowers, or the way other people look out for each other as they navigate crowded streets, to name but a few.

As you notice these positive things, acknowledge each one in your mind—don't let them just slip past you. Pause for a moment as you really see, hear, or sense each thing, and make sure it registers in your conscious awareness. Really take it in. Try to identify what it is about each thing that makes it pleasurable to you.

While walking, try to take a different route each day, so that you do not become too accustomed to any of these things and start to take them for granted. If you are with a loved one, take turns pointing out and explaining why something you see is positive. Observe, soak in, and discuss the blessings of life around you and the positive things that happened in your day; do this before starting to vent about any frustrations.

Again, Wilson (2016) reports, "[Gratitude conversations occur] when people intentionally engage in conversation with others about positive events, experiences, or outcomes that happen each day. By expressing gratitude about these events, people broaden and build their social bonds with others, which leads to community strength and harmony (Fredrickson, 2004)" (p. 3).

REMEMBERING THE BAD

Reflection is a powerful process. I thoroughly enjoy life. And I thoroughly enjoy my life. Therefore, fully aware, but not quite able to fully embrace the idea, I understand that tomorrow is promised to no one. As I reflect back on my life—my journey—I cannot help but be grateful; I know that everything and every experience from this day forward is simply gravy—a bonus. I know this to be true, because regardless of X, Y, or Z, life is good. It is with this realization that I share the final gratitude practice. Although there are more practices that could be shared, the practice of remembering the bad has been a reservoir of gratitude for me over the years

Remembering the bad is when you remember how difficult life used to be and how far you have come. In an online article, Robert Emmons (2013) explains remembering the bad in this way:

> Think of the worst times in your life, your sorrows, your losses, your sadness—and then remember that here you are, able to remember them, that you made it through the worst times of your life, you got through the trauma, you got through the trial, you endured the temptation, you survived the bad relationship, you're making your way out of the dark. Remember the bad things, then look to see where you are now.
>
> This process of remembering how difficult life used to be and how far we have come sets up an explicit contrast that is fertile ground for gratefulness. Our minds think in terms of counter-factuals—mental comparisons we make between the way things are and how things might have been different. Contrasting the present with negative times in the past can make us feel happier (or at least less unhappy) and enhance our overall sense of well-being. This opens the door to coping [with life] gratefully.

As the saying goes, "So far I've survived 100 percent of my worst days. This too shall pass." As an assistant principal, I often operated from this mindset. After a day of dealing with issues ranging from students fighting to students being taken to the hospital in an ambulance from overdosing on drugs to lockdowns to being handed a hand grenade, I would often say to my colleagues, "The day always ends.

No matter what, I am either going to bed at some point or I am dead. Either way, the day is going to end." When dealing with difficult and stressful situations, this mindset has helped me to view my current reality as temporary.

Therefore, think about a difficult time in your life. When you contrast that time to the present, do you feel grateful? Why? How? Does it make you realize that your current situation is not as bad as it could be? Then, try to recognize and appreciate how good your life is now. As Emmons (2013) says, "The point is not to ignore or forget the past but to develop a fruitful frame of reference in the present from which to view experiences and events."

As shared in Chapter 6, regarding my wife and me, remembering the early days of our marriage and the journey we were on together while I was becoming a teacher—including driving that 1967 Ford Mustang—is a great avenue for remembering the bad. Although it was a difficult time, we survived it. Not only did we survive but we also learned many life lessons and created some great memories that led to hilarious stories, and we now have a greater appreciation for each other, and even for all the "things" we have accumulated and experienced together.

TODAY'S REALITY DOES NOT DEFINE TOMORROW'S REALITY

I will end this book how I started: by discussing how awesome it was growing up in the eighties. As a child, I played all day, and well into the night with little to no adult supervision. Early in the morning, I would ride off from my house on my bike and would not return until the sun went down. With little to no rules governing my actions, my independence grew every year.

As I got older, my parents had only two rules, one of which was spoken, and the other unspoken. The spoken rule was that I must maintain a 3.0 grade point average (GPA) in order to drive, as a 3.0

GPA brought a discount in my car insurance. The unspoken rule was that I not get arrested. Regarding the spoken rule: I graduated from high school with exactly a 3.0 GPA—no more, and no less. Regarding the unspoken rule: I never got arrested. However, just because someone does not get arrested does not mean that they do not get into trouble.

In the second grade, my teacher wrote a letter to my parents that I still have to this day. It was dated January 1, 1978, and it read, "Mr. and Mrs. Barlow. Marc and I have discussed his behavior at school so I feel that Marc understands how he 'should' behave. I thought that you would be interested in the report I've had from another teacher and from what I have observed. Marc seems to be 'feeling his oats' lately and has taken to using the 'F' word on the playground. Also, his participation in Judo has given him the feeling that he can flip other children because he has the correct knowledge. He has also been in trouble in the cafeteria for misbehaving and on the playground for rough-housing. He knows how he should behave and I have spoken to him about taking responsibility for his behaviors."

Although my behavior leveled out somewhat as I got older, my apathy toward school increased steadily over the years. Still, I must have shown some type of promise in high school because I was chosen to be in honors classes and was selected by the staff—and was first runner-up—for Boys State, which is a leadership and citizenship program sponsored by the American Legion and the American Legion Auxiliary for high school juniors. Furthermore, my peers must have also thought highly of me, as I was nominated to be on the Homecoming Court. Nevertheless, my apathy reached its zenith and became tangible during the Homecoming festivities.

During Homecoming Week, the school put up pictures of the entire Homecoming Court, with a list of each student's accomplishments underneath their picture. For example, under the picture of Student

X, it would read, "Student X: Varsity basketball, football, and baseball; 3.8 GPA; Honor Roll all four years"; under the picture of Student Y it would read, "Student Y: Varsity baseball all four years; 4.0 GPA; ASB Vice President"; and so on. Then it came to me and my picture, where it read, "Marc Barlow: Senior." My apathy was now tangible for all to see. I had risked very little, and, as a result, had accomplished very little. I very much had the fixed mindset. The reason I went into education was because of my chemistry teacher; ironically, his class was the only class I failed in high school.

Let me paint you a picture of one incident to describe the type of student I was, particularly in that chemistry class. I had chemistry right after lunch, and the teacher was in his second year of teaching. One day, as the teacher briefly stepped out of the classroom, I decided to pick up a Bunsen burner and throw it across the room to startle my friend, whom I called my "partner in crime." The teacher had already separated us, which is why I was throwing the Bunsen burner across the room.

I'll never forget that day—that exact moment, in fact—when the Bunsen burner was literally about to leave my hand when, I saw, in my peripheral vision, the teacher walk back into the classroom. With the Bunsen burner already in the air, all I could do was wait and watch (with the teacher) as it hurtled across the classroom and crashed against the wall. This was who I was in high school.

Although I had less than a 20 percent in my chemistry class, the teacher did not kick me out. Rather, he spoke life over me, and began calling out all of the positive things he saw in me; things I had never seen in myself. He saw more in me than I saw in myself. Even to this day, I still get overwhelmed with emotion when I think about how he made me feel about myself. With the wisdom of a teacher (combined with the ignorance of a young, adolescent boy), he told me that if I could pass the final, I would pass the class.

It was only very recently that I realized he had totally tricked me. After all, what were the chances that a student who always messed around—one who had less than a 20 percent average—could ever pass the final? It was brilliant. Although not aware of the terrible odds against me at the time, I respected him for the opportunity of redemption. As one would expect, I failed the final, and thus, failed the class. Regardless, he changed the trajectory of my life. To my shame, it took me 12 years—during my seventh year of teaching—to finally reach out via email to let him know the impact he had had on my life.

Back then, however, I still had a debt to pay for my apathy. Several years after graduating from high school, as I finally got serious about pursuing my education, I enrolled in a community college. The final bill for this apathy debt came with the results of my college placement exams. For English, I scored so low that I was required to take two remedial English courses before I could enroll in the actual English course I needed for college and to transfer the credit. It was even worse for math. For math, I scored so low that I was required to take three remedial math courses before I could enroll in the math course I needed for college and to transfer the credit.

But, you know what? I made it. It was hard. I struggled. I had to grow up and own up. But I made it. In retrospect, a major reason I got through was the change in my mindset. I developed a growth mindset where I embraced challenges, persisted in the face of obstacles, and was able to see my effort as a path to mastery.

The lesson is it is never too late. Do not succumb to the "unconscious holdover" of your old paradigm—your old ways of thinking—and listen to the lies in your head telling you that you are too old, too far in debt, too lazy, not smart enough, or any other falsity that stands in the way of your goals of being debt and financially free and the best, healthiest version of yourself. You are the only one who can redesign the reality of both your life and your finances. It all begins with you.

Today. Right now. Go. You've got this.

Once again, becoming disciplined and planning for your future is paramount in redesigning the reality of your finances. Therefore, no matter how much money you make, if you need assistance in creating and sticking to concrete plans in order to get out—and stay out—of debt, then please visit redesignthereality.com for more information.

TO LEARN MORE, PLEASE VISIT:

redesignthereality.com
facebook.com/redesignthereality

TO CONNECT WITH MARC, PLEASE EMAIL:

info@redesignthereality.com
redesignthereality@gmail.com

RESOURCES

Chapter 1
Aristotle. (n.d.). Aristotle quotes. *BrainyQuote*. Retrieved from www.brainyquote.com/quotes/aristotle_100584.

Chapter 3
Gandhi, M. (n.d.). Mahatma Gandhi quotes. *BrainyQuote*. Retrieved from www.brainyquote.com/quotes/mahatma_gandhi_109075.

Morpheus – The Matrix: Quotes. (n.d.). *Goodreads*. Retrieved from www.goodreads.com/author/quotes/7392901.Morpheus_The_Matrix.

Silver, J. (Producer), & The Wachowski Brothers (Directors). (1999). *The Matrix* [Motion picture]. U.S.: Village Roadshow Films.

Chapter 4
ACEs science 101. (n.d.). *ACEs Too High*. Retrieved from acestoohigh.com/aces-101/.

Got your ACE score? (n.d.). *ACEs Too High*. Retrieved from acestoohigh.com/got-your-ace-score/.

Office of Superintendent of Public Instruction. Learning and Teaching Support. Compassionate Schools. (2016). Learning and teaching support. Retrieved from k12.wa.us/CompassionateSchools/

HeartofLearning.aspx.

Stevens, J. E. (2015). The adverse childhood experiences study: The largest, most important public health study you never heard of – began in an obesity clinic. *ACEs Too High*. Retrieved from acestoohigh.com/2012/10/03/the-adverse-childhood-experiences-study-the-largest-most-important-public-health-study-you-never-heard-of-began-in-an-obesity-clinic/.

Chapter 5

California Department of Education. (2016). Smarter balanced assessment test results for: State of California; 2016 state smarter balanced results. Retrieved from caaspp.cde.ca.gov/sb2017/ViewReport?ps=true&lstTestYear=2016&lstTestType=B&lstCounty=00&lstDistrict=00000&lstSchool=0000000&lstGrade=4.

Goff, B. (2014). *Love does: Discover a secretly incredible life in an ordinary world.* Nashville, TN: Thomas Nelson.

Harrington, T. (2017). Until poverty eliminated, schools won't graduate 100 percent of students, expert says. *EdSource*. Retrieved from edsource.org/2017/poverty-poses-obstacle-to-100-percent-graduation-rate-expert-says/589190?utm_source=newsletter&utm_medium=email.

National Center for Education Statistics. (2013). Digest of education statistics. Retrieved from nces.ed.gov/programs/digest/d13/tables/dt13_219.70.asp.

Rumberger, R. W. (2013). Poverty and high school dropouts: The impact of family and community poverty on high school dropouts.

Retrieved from www.apa.org/pi/ses/resources/indicator/2013/05/poverty-dropouts.aspx.

Silvernail, D. L., Sloan, J. E., Paul, C. R., Johnson, A. F., & Stump, E. K. (2014). The relationship between school poverty and student achievement in Maine [Brief]. Portland, ME: University of Southern Maine, Center for Education Policy, Applied Research and Evaluation.

U.S. Bureau of Labor Statistics. (2015). Median weekly earnings by educational attainment in 2014. Retrieved from www.bls.gov/opub/ted/2015/median-weekly-earnings-by-education-gender-race-and-ethnicity-in-2014.htm.

Chapter 6

Duckworth, A. L. (2013, April). Grit: The power of passion and perseverance [Video file]. Retrieved from www.ted.com/talks/angela_lee_duckworth_grit_the_power_of_passion_and_perseverance#t-191271.

Chapter 7

Dweck, C. S. (2006). *Mindset: The new psychology of success*. New York, NY: Ballantine Books.

Marsh, J. (2013, February 20). Debunking the myths of happiness. *Greater Good Magazine*. Retrieved from greatergood.berkeley.edu/article/item/sonja_lyubomirsky_on_the_myths_of_happiness.

Tarnas, R. (2001). A new birth in freedom: A (p)review of Jorge Ferrer's revisioning transpersonal theory. A participatory vision of human spirituality. *Journal of Transpersonal Psychology, 33*(1), 64–71.

Chapter 8
Howells, K. (2012). *Gratitude in education: A radical view.* Rotterdam, The Netherlands: Sense Publishers.

Practice. (n.d.). *Google [search].* Retrieved from https://www.google.com/search?q=practice&oq=practi&aqs=chrome.0.69i59j69i-57j0l4.2135j1j7&sourceid=chrome&ie=UTF-8.

Chapter 9
Murray, T. D. (2016, January 14). Why do 70 percent of lottery winners end up bankrupt? *Cleveland.com.* Retrieved from www.cleveland.com/business/index.ssf/2016/01/why_do_70_percent_of_lottery_w.html.

Ramsey, D. (2011). *Dave Ramsey's complete guide to money: The handbook of Financial Peace University.* Brentwood, TN: Lampo Press.

Chapter 10
Debt repayment calculator. (n.d.). *Credit Karma.* Retrieved from www.creditkarma.com/calculators/debtrepayment.

Roth IRA calculator. (n.d.). *Bankrate.* Retrieved from www.bankrate.com/calculators/retirement/roth-ira-plan-calculator.

Chapter 11
Amazen U. (2017). *Mind in a jar* [Video file]. Retrieved from www.youtube.com/watch?v=P2SqvqcQ__o.

Emmons, R. (2013, November 12). What gets in the way of gratitude? *Greater Good Magazine.* Retrieved from greatergood.berkeley.edu/article/item/what_stops_gratitude.

Fisk, M. (2013). McKenzie Fisk: About the artist. Retrieved from mckenziefisk.com/artist/.

Kabat-Zinn, J. (2013). *What Is mindfulness?* [Video file]. Retrieved from www.youtube.com/watch?v=HmEo6RI4Wvs.

Mindfulness defined: What is mindfulness? (n.d.). *Greater Good Magazine*. Retrieved from greatergood.berkeley.edu/topic/mindfulness/definition.

The importance of knowing yourself. (n.d.). *Habits for Wellbeing*. Retrieved from www.habitsforwellbeing.com/importance-knowing.

Chapter 12

Auto Loan Amortization Calculator. (2018) myAmortizationChart.com. Retrieved from www.myamortizationchart.com/auto-loan-amortization-calculator/.

Auto loan calculator: Estimate your monthly car payment. (2017). *NerdWallet*. Retrieved from www.nerdwallet.com/blog/loans/car-loan-calculator/.

Staermose, S. (Producer), & Oplev, N. A. (Director). (2010). *The Girl with the Dragon Tattoo* [Motion picture]. Sweden: Music Box Films.

The Girl with the Dragon Tattoo: Quotes. (n.d.). *IMDb*. Retrieved from www.imdb.com/title/tt1568346/quotes.

Chapter 13

Blocker, D., Hildebrand, F., & Kelly, J. J. (Producers), & Penn, S. (Director). (2008). *Into the wild* [Motion picture]. U.S.: Paramount Home Entertainment.

Emmons, R. (2010, November 16). Why gratitude is good. *Greater Good Magazine*. Retrieved from greatergood.berkeley.edu/article/item/why_gratitude_is_good.

Gratitude defined: What is gratitude? (n.d.). *Greater Good Magazine*. Retrieved from greatergood.berkeley.edu/topic/gratitude/definition#why_practice.

Krakauer, J. (n.d.). Jon Krakauer: quotes; quotable quote. Goodreads. Retrieved from www.goodreads.com/quotes/95356-when-you-forgive-you-love-and-when-you-love-god-s.

Maciulskis, K. (2013). *2 tigers and the monk: Past, future, present* [Video file]. Retrieved from www.youtube.com/watch?v=Yj2pUhS_S6U.

Sáenz, A. (2012). *The power of a teacher*. Peoria: AZ: Intermedia Publishing Group.

Sher, M. L. (2013, December 8). Don't drink poison. *The Huffington Post*. Retrieved from www.huffingtonpost.com/margery-leveen-sher/dont-drink-poison_b_4408347.html.

The 31 benefits of gratitude you didn't know about: How gratitude can change your life. (n.d.). *Happier Human*. Retrieved from happierhuman.com/benefits-of-gratitude/.

Twain, M. (n.d.). Mark Twain quotes. *BrainyQuote*. Retrieved from www.brainyquote.com/quotes/mark_twain_100631

Ward, W. A. (n.d.). William Arthur Ward quotes. *BrainyQuote*. Retrieved from www.brainyquote.com/quotes/william_arthur_ward_676240.

Wilson, J. T. (2016). Brightening the mind: The impact of practicing gratitude on focus and resilience in learning. *Journal of the Scholarship of Teaching and Learning, 16*(4), 1–13.doi: 10.14434/josotl.v16i4.19998. Retrieved from https://josotl.indiana.edu/article/view/19998.

Chapter 14

Emmons, R. (2010, November 17). 10 ways to become more grateful. *Greater Good Magazine*. Retrieved from greatergood.berkeley.edu/article/item/ten_ways_to_become_more_grateful1/.

Emmons, R. (2013, May 13). How gratitude can help you through hard times. *Greater Good Magazine*. Retrieved from greatergood.berkeley.edu/article/item/how_gratitude_can_help_you_through_hard_times.

Greater Good in action: Gratitude journal. (n.d.). Retrieved from ggia.berkeley.edu/practice/gratitude_journal#.

Greater Good in action: Gratitude letter. (n.d.). Retrieved from ggia.berkeley.edu/practice/gratitude_letter.

Greater Good in action: Mental subtraction of positive events. (n.d.). Retrieved from ggia.berkeley.edu/practice/mental_subtraction_positive_events.

Greater Good in action: Savoring walk. (n.d.). Retrieved from ggia.berkeley.edu/practice/savoring_walk.

Made in the USA
San Bernardino, CA
06 December 2018